# Salt in His Blood

# Salt in His Blood

## The Life of Michael De Ruyter

William R. Rang

INHERITANCE PUBLICATIONS
NEERLANDIA, ALBERTA, CANADA
PELLA, IOWA, U.S.A.

**Canadian Cataloguing in Publication Data**
Rang, William R.
Salt in his blood

ISBN 0-921100-59-0
1. Ruyter, Michiel Adriaanszoon de, 1607-1676. 2. Admirals—Netherlands—Biography. 3. Netherlands—History, Naval. I. Title.
DJ136.R8R36 1996 949.2'04'092 C96-910688-2

**Library of Congress Cataloging-in-Publication Data**
Rang, William R., 1926-
Salt in his blood : the life of Michael De Ruyter / William R. Rang
p. cm.
Summary: A fictionalized biography of Michael De Ruyter, the skillful and courageous seventeenth-century Dutch admiral who tried to live his life according to Christian principles.
ISBN 0-921100-59-0
1. Ruyter, Michiel Adriaanszoon de, 1607-1676—Juvenile fiction. 2. Netherlands—History, Naval—Juvenile fiction. [1. De Ruyter, Michael, 1607-1676—Fiction. 2. Netherlands—History, Naval—Fiction. 3. Sea stories. 4. Christian life—Fiction.] I. Title.
PZ7.R163Sal 1996
[Fic]—dc21 96-39179
CIP
AC

Illustrations taken from old Dutch books.
Cover Picture: Johannes Kollaard (Used with friendly permission of Den Hertog, B.V. - Houten/Utrecht, The Netherlands)

2nd Printing 2006

All rights reserved © 1996, 2006 by Inheritance Publications
Box 154, Neerlandia, Alberta Canada T0G 1R0
Tel. (780) 674 3949
Web site: http://www.telusplanet.net/public/inhpubl/webip/ip.htm
E-Mail inhpubl@telusplanet.net

Published simultaneously in U.S.A. by Inheritance Publications
Box 366, Pella, Iowa 50219

Available in Australia from Inheritance Publications
Box 1122, Kelmscott, W.A. 6111 Tel. & Fax (089) 390 4940

Printed in Canada

*With thanks to my son Lloyd*
*who lovingly and carefully guided*
*this book to completion.*

# *Literature*

Blok, P., *The Life of Admiral de Ruyter*,
Westport, CT., Greenwood Press, 1975

Brandt, Gerard, *Het leven en bedrijf van den Heere Michiel de Ruiter*, Amsterdam, 1687

De Zeeuw, P., *Michiel Adriaansz. de Ruyter*,
G.B. Van Goor, 1957

Norel, K., *Bestevaer*,
Zwolle, La Riviere & Voorhoeve, 1957

Roelink J., *Vlissinger Michiel*,
Nijkerk, Callenbach N.V., 1957

Van der Leeden, P., *Bestevaer Michiel*,
Kampen, J.H. Kok, 1957

# Contents

*Michiel Adriaanszoon De Ruyter (1607-1676)*
[Michael, son of Adrian, the Rider]

# CHAPTER ONE

## *A RESTLESS BOY*

The lashing wind and the beating rain that drenched the Dutch port town of Flushing made it miserable to be outside, but the boys leaning against the brick wall of an old warehouse didn't mind. The wild wind was no stranger to them. Their clothes were soaked and water trickled down their faces.

It was the year 1618, and it had been raining year in, year out for as long as any of these boys could remember. If they had asked their parents, they would have found that they, too, remembered few truly sunny days. The boys stood with their hands deep in their pockets. None of them spoke, but one boy whistled between his teeth. It was a merry little tune that sounded silly in the rain, but he didn't care. He, too, was waiting. They all knew for whom they were waiting. A few more minutes and then the harbour boys would pass on their way home. There would be a fight again.

This street belonged to the biggest of the waiting boys: the Rat. Other boys were not allowed to pass. After the fight there would be torn clothes and fat lips, but they didn't worry about it too much. The Rat's boys were taller than the harbour boys. The other advantage was that they had the Rat as a leader, and the Rat knew how to fight.

"They're scared. They won't show up," one of the boys finally remarked, lazily.

The Rat grinned. He had a built-in space between his two front teeth. "Of course they won't come. We might as well go home, I guess. They know whose street this is." He looked at one of his friends, but nobody could ever be sure whether the Rat was really looking at him or not. His eyes seemed to look in two directions at once.

"Wait," another boy shouted. "I hear them coming."

The Rat scowled. Those harbour boys had some nerve, walking on his street. He slowly extended his enormous fists out of the sleeves of his coat. "Ready?"

The other boys clenched their fists, scowling. Ready! Anytime, Rat!

A group of six boys came around the corner of the street. They walked side by side with their hands in their pockets and their shoulders pulled up. Their leader was short, but powerfully built for his size. Michael De Ruyter walked in the middle of the group: a broad-shouldered youngster with messy dark hair and darting brown eyes. He walked stiffly, his short strong legs confidently carving up the cobblestones. Spreading his thick arms wide he stopped his friends.

"Wait a minute," he said calmly. He measured the distance separating the two gangs. Then he noticed the Rat. Michael stared defiantly at him.

"Michael is with them," one of the Rat's friends said in almost a whisper. The Rat didn't want to show that he, too, felt uneasy. He just shrugged his shoulders. "My fists are ready," he responded, but his voice quavered. Yet, he was the leader, and, to demonstrate it, he made one small step forward out of the line of boys.

"What are you doing here on my street? Are you looking for a fight?" he shouted.

"We're just minding our business," Michael replied, "we're not here to pick a fight. That's all you're after. We just want to go home, that's all. 'Your' street is on our way home." He paused. "But if you want to stop us, just try." He placed his hands on his hips and waited.

The Rat hadn't expected this. He looked at his friends for their opinions, but not one of them said a word. Then he looked at Michael again. "This is our street. We're not letting you through."

"If that's what you want, it's fine with us!" Michael shot back. Sprinting like a cat, he raced forward, followed by his pals. The Rat was at the middle of the line of thugs. Michael went straight for him. The Rat lifted his mighty right arm and swung wildly, but his aim was poor and Michael ducked, missing the impact of the powerful fist by just a few inches. Then Michael jumped on his opponent's back. While his left hand firmly grabbed the Rat's hair, his right hand pounded away like a woodpecker at the big boy's eyes and nose. Because of the sudden impact the Rat lost his balance and fell backwards. Michael was on his chest, still hammering away.

"Get off!" the Rat wailed. "I . . . I . . ."

Michael stopped immediately. "Had enough?" he asked, looking around. Where were his friends? Gone in pursuit, probably. He let the Rat go.

"O.K." he said threateningly, his eyes glimmering like polished armour. He stood up and looked at his pants. There were two big holes in the knees where they had scraped the cobblestones. It occurred to him that his mother would be upset about this, but Michael realized that he had to worry about this later. Without looking back at the Rat he walked away. He stopped at the street corner, put two fingers of his right hand under his tongue and sent a shrill whistle into the rain-laden air. Now his friends would know that they could stop. The battle was over.

Slowly the Rat came to his feet. His eyes were swollen and his nose bled badly. He groaned and felt his mouth with his stubby fingers.

No wonder his mouth felt strange. Michael had hammered his two front teeth out.

* * *

Michael went the rest of the way home without his friends. Although the rain had stopped, the streets were still glimmering and wet. He stepped hard in a puddle or two, splashing the water in every direction. Another fight. He would have to explain to his father that he had not provoked the other boys. His father had made it clear more than once that he didn't want his son to go around picking fights. "When you do that, you show a lack of character," he had said. "And certainly don't fight with boys who are smaller than you are." Michael had nodded in agreement then but realized now how hypocritical that would seem to his father. His mother, on the other hand, would be upset because of his torn pants. She had told him so often to be careful with his clothes since his father was only a dock worker. The family was poor.

Despite what his parents said, Michael enjoyed the odd fight. School was a chore and his frequent visits to the harbour were only really exciting when ships came in from the East.

As he entered another street, he slowed his pace. He would have to look into his mother's eyes, and every time he did that, he felt like slinking away like a puppy. His mother would look hurt; more hurt than the Rat, or any other boy he had pummelled with his fists, had been.

His footfalls echoed distinctly in the street where he lived. It must have been later than he thought for it had begun to darken. The lamplighter had already made his rounds. And Father would be home for sure. He would be seated in his big chair, which was the family's only luxury, and he would be waiting.

The young fighter slowed his steps. He was ten years old now and was already a bit of a problem child. His younger brothers and sisters behaved much better than he did. People came often to the small home of Adrian Michielszoon's family to complain about the "little rascal." Michael knew he was a ruffian and wasn't proud of it. He wished he could change but it was so difficult! What would his father say this time? Would he understand that his son had only been defending himself? The best thing was to speak up and to explain everything. There was no use lying about it. His father hated lying and so did Michael. Except the part about enjoying the fight. He didn't think he could explain *that* to his father.

He unlatched the door and stole into the little kitchen. The oil lamp was turned low and this made it hard to see the expression on his father's face. His mother wasn't there. She was probably putting his brothers and sisters to bed.

"Good evening, Father," Michael began as he closed the door behind him. Despite his earlier intention to be straightforward, he hoped that his father didn't notice anything unusual.

Adrian Michielszoon didn't reply. He sat there and watched. Michael didn't know what to do. He saw his father get up slowly. Now he wished he could leave the kitchen and run to the shelter of his bed under the roof in the attic.

Finally, a deep voice spoke. "You're late. Where have you been all this time?"

Michael cleared his throat. "I've been around with some of my friends, that's all."

"Have you been fighting again?"

Michael nodded imperceptibly. "I was."

His father rose and walked right up to his son. The boy's head just reached to his father's chest. He suddenly felt quite small.

"Listen, Son," he began. "I've punished you often, and many a time I've spanked you so hard that you could hardly sit any more. And every time you promised me something. Remember?"

Michael nodded. He remembered his promises. He had promised to stop fighting, but somehow he just couldn't help himself.

"It's so hard to change!" The words burst out like a torrent.

"That's because you've tried to change yourself all by yourself. You know that this will never work. You must ask the Lord to change you. When you ask, He will."

"Yes, I know." Michael had known it all along, but somehow he had neglected prayer. That's why nothing had happened.

"You have disappointed me again, Son. You have also displeased the Lord. Now I must do something about it again."

Michael put his hands on his rump. That's where he expected the punishment to land. Hard.

"When did you get your last spanking?" his father asked.

Michael looked up silently. He knew too well that it wasn't all that long ago.

His father waited for an answer but when Michael didn't reply, he continued. "Spanking doesn't help any more, does it? Maybe going to bed without supper will be a more effective punishment. Go before I change my mind!"

Michael's eyes went wide. He couldn't believe it. "Yes, uh . . . good night, Father." He fled the kitchen.

A few minutes later Mother came in. "Where is Michael, Adrian?" she asked.

Adrian took his chair. "I sent him to bed without supper. Just like that. Spanking doesn't help any more. It used to, a little . . ."

His wife didn't reply. With a sigh she picked up the socks that needed mending.

They sat for a long time without speaking. The silent evening hours crept by. When the light of the oil-lamp grew dim, both went to bed.

Before they went to sleep, however, Father and Mother prayed. Much of their supplication concerned their feisty little boy. "O Lord, please use him. In some way, please let him be fruitful in Thy service."

# CHAPTER TWO

## *THE SEA*

The next morning Michael got up extra early. No wonder: his stomach was grumbling as he woke. He dressed himself quickly, climbed over his snoring younger brothers and sisters, and slid down the ladder into the kitchen. His mother wasn't there, but to judge by the loaf of bread on the table, his father had gone to work already. He scanned the room for the pail of water that his mother always put there, but she hadn't pumped one yet.

Never mind, he would do it himself. It would save her some work. As the pump creaked, the cool water filled the pail. Michael thrust his head in it. That made him feel better! Now he was wide awake. As he took the towel to dry his face, his mother came in. She took the loaf of bread, held it against her stomach, and using the mean looking knife that was lying there, she sliced a chunk for him.

"Good morning, Mother," Michael began.

"Good morning," she replied, taking a seat at the table. "You're early."

Michael faked a smile. "That's because I'm hungry, I guess."

His mother nodded. She knew that her growing boy had a huge appetite. It wasn't easy for them to feed the twelve[1] children, especially with Michael's appetite.

---

[1] Michael (or Michiel) was the fourth child of Adrian Michielszoon and Alida Jans van Middelburgh, (also called Alida De Ruyter [the rider, or, the horseman] since her father [or brother] was a horseman in the army of Prince Maurice of Nassau). He had four brothers and six sisters, and a half sister from his father's first marriage.

After he had given thanks, he began eating his piece of bread in silence. Then he stood up, holding the bread.

"You're much too early for school, Michael," his mother observed.

"I know," he replied between bites, stuffing bits of bread that were falling out of his mouth back in with his fingers. "You see, I'd like to go to the harbour to take a look at one of Seigneur Lampsens' ships. It's supposed to leave for Liverpool today."

"You're going there again?" His mother's tone was disapproving, but Michael seemed to miss it.

"Of course! The sailors are always so full of stories and the ships sometimes sail with their gun-ports open. Can you imagine what it must be like to travel all over the world?" What he didn't say was how much more he enjoyed the harbour than his classroom.

"I know," she replied. "But you won't get far if you don't study in school. Captains need a lot of learning. Would you like to be a captain?"

"Of course. I'm going to be a captain!"

His mother smiled. "In that case you'll want to go to school and be there on time."

Michael nodded. She was right, but wasn't there an easier way?

His mother stood and moved beside him. "Michael?"

He looked up and met her eyes. "Yes, Mother?"

"Don't forget to go to school today, will you, please? You just can't go on like this. You know it."

"Yes, but . . . I don't like school, I hate it!" Michael struck the table with his fist as he spat out the words.

If his mother was surprised by his outburst she chose not to react. "I want you to try because of me, Michael. You need school, you need to learn many things. I really want you to try."

He squirmed. "Yes, Mother." He spoke the words too quickly, he knew. He just wanted to end the conversation.

He gave his mother a swift kiss and darted out the door. As he ran down the street the sounds of his wooden shoes clattered against the little houses on either side.

Then he stopped momentarily. The masts of some ships at port rose above the roofs of the houses. One ship had very high masts. Michael knew that there was a man-o-war in the harbour. It must have come in during the night. He turned one more corner before coming to the port. This was life! Suddenly he forgot his conversation with his mother and he forgot about school. He wished he could sail this very day! He was old enough and many boys of his age sailed already. At one time he had talked about it at home, but his parents had not answered. Father had been a sailor once, but he had said that a sailor's life wasn't good for a man who had a family. It was dangerous and rough. Many ships never returned; they either sank during storms or were captured by pirates.

He leaned against an oily oaken barrel and watched a ship being loaded. The men looked so healthy and so strong! One rolled a cask bigger than himself. Another sailor on the dock was obviously the skipper. He made sure that the ship was loaded properly. It wouldn't be long before it would set sail. Michael knew from experience that the wind was favourable. Boy, he wished he could jump on board . . .

"No school for you today, lad?" A deep voice behind him alarmed him. Turning around he locked eyes with Seigneur Lampsens himself, a tall, round-faced man. No wonder he was stout for his height; he was the owner of a successful shipping firm and could afford good food.

"Sir . . . yes, Sir. I forgot," he stammered. Michael snapped out of his reverie and ran. Was he ever forgetful! And his mother had asked him to try harder.

When he entered the half-dark classroom, the lessons had started already. He went straight to the teacher's table.

"I'm late, Sir," he began.

The grizzled schoolmaster looked up. "I'm late, I'm late. That's all Michael Adrianszoon has to say for himself. It's all he ever says. But he does not tell why he is late. He has been daydreaming again, and he has forgotten that he needed the school to rid him of bad habits. You're fifteen minutes late this time. That's one slap with the strap for every three minutes. Five strokes with the strap you will receive right now. Put your hand up!"

Michael obeyed. He knew that being late was usually followed by the strap. How often had the teacher used the strap on his hands already, Michael wondered.

The strap came down hard. Sharp pain flashed up his whole arm. Michael didn't cry. Boys should not cry, he knew. He wanted to be tough like his father. Whenever he received the strap, he would always think of the sea. Each stroke became a slippery rope in his hand, a rope that almost tore off his skin. He locked eyes with the teacher. All through the punishment, he glared at him.

"Sit down," the teacher commanded after the final stroke with the strap. "We are busy with arithmetic. The other boys have already completed some of their sums. You must stay after school to finish your work. Before you start, you must tell me how much six times eight makes. Can you remember?"

Michael looked up, blankly, his hand still smarting. He didn't remember. He had not paid any attention to the teacher the day before, and he wasn't going to pay any attention now either.

# CHAPTER THREE

## *SCHOOL*

"I can't remember, Sir," he replied.

"Can't remember, can't remember! You never remember anything I have taught you. You always forget. How often have I told you that people only forget the things they don't want to remember? Get to work. Right now!" The veins in his teacher's neck were throbbing. He was serious!

Michael obeyed. The old teacher was right. Michael didn't pay attention to things that didn't interest him, and school was one of those things. What was the use of knowing how much six times eight was? Ships were more important. A good sailor didn't need to know all of that school stuff. A school? Four high walls with barely a window in them. Real life existed outside the walls.

Michael stared at his work. He managed to write down a few answers on his black slate, but his mind was on board the ships. Would Seigneur Lampsens' ship be ready to leave port, he wondered? He looked at the teacher without seeing him. Instead, he saw a ship. A fine, old, tall ship with big gray sails.

Suddenly he woke up from his daydreaming, but it was too late to catch what the teacher had just said. Peter Jansz, who was sitting in front of him, hadn't missed the point. He never missed anything. Michael hated the way Peter always sat, ramrod straight, eyes focused only on the teacher.

Michael studied the back of his classmate attentively. Suddenly a wild idea came to him. He produced a piece of rope from his pocket. Grinning to himself, he bent carefully forward to reach the boy's ankle. Soundlessly, he fastened the rope to the boy's seat and, with a rapid movement of his nimble fingers, he tied the other end to Pete's ankle. Michael straightened himself and waited. As usual, the teacher would ask Peter to come to his desk. This time, it would cause some commotion.

"Michael Adrianszoon, come and show me your work."

This was unexpected. Michael stood up. As he passed Peter, he gave him a hard slap on the shoulder. Peter would retaliate, Michael knew.

It was like someone had put fire to a keg of gunpowder. Peter furiously leapt up after Michael. But he didn't get very far. There was a crash. The teacher's prize pupil fell to the floor. A water bottle fell from the desk and rolled along, emptying itself generously. The other boys jumped up to see what had caused the commotion.

Michael stood, doubled over, in front of the class. His hands were pressed hard against his stomach. Tears rolled down his cheeks. He had never laughed so much in all his life!

His fun didn't last very long. "You did it, didn't you?" The teacher's veins were throbbing again, this time even the ones on his forehead stood out. He turned to pick up his stick.

Michael knew what that meant. He knew from experience what the teacher was going to do with his hickory stick. Like a flash he jumped over his fallen classmate and dashed out of the room. Moments later he was outside.

Michael sprinted toward the harbour, breathing the fresh salty air in deep, satisfied breaths. He hoped that Seigneur Lampsens' ship would still be there.

Disappointment awaited him. The ship had just departed. Michael could still see it. Until they got to the high seas, ships moved like snails on a log. Nevertheless, he had missed the farewell ceremonies, the all-important handshake between the captain and Seigneur Lampsens. He was too late. He could still see the ship, but that wasn't enough. He wanted to see everything just as if he were on board himself. He wanted to watch it for as long as possible. And he could do that if he stood on something higher off the ground.

Michael looked around. What about the roof of one of the houses?

It would take only a minute for him to climb that high. It wasn't a bad idea, but a roof was still too low. He needed something higher than a roof.

His eyes wandered around. Then a daring idea struck him. The church tower, of course! He knew that the tower was under repair and that the workers had put up scaffolds which would make the climb much easier. It was almost noon now. The workers wouldn't be there to stop him.

It didn't take Michael long to make up his mind. The church was only a block away from where he stood. Within minutes he was climbing the poles of the scaffolds. Nobody noticed him. Seeing no ladders, he worked his way up on the poles. He didn't mind. Climbing poles was as easy for him as walking up stairs or shinning up ladders.

At the second platform he took a little rest. He was quite high above the street already. Now he could also see the harbour better and could clearly see Lampsens' ship!

Higher and higher he went. His view became even more magnificent. This was fun!

Soon he reached the highest scaffold. Here he paused for a minute. Was his view ever splendid! The houses and the ships were puny now. The people looked like insects. Never before had he been this high off the street nor had he looked that far across the water. It was as if the ships didn't move at all.

After a few minutes Michael didn't like his spot any more. He hadn't reached the highest point of the tower yet, but he could not go much higher. There was only the big, brass sphere. It wouldn't offer him a good place to sit. But wait, there was the weather vane. That was the highest point!

He climbed the round sphere and with a firm grip he took hold of the strong steel bar to which the weather vane was fastened. He put his legs around the bar and set himself. This was it! He had reached the highest point on the earth!

Little spheres of starlight danced in his eyes as he watched the scenery below him. Never before had the world looked so beautiful to him, and never before had the sea seemed more attractive or more inviting. He realized it stronger than ever. In those narrow streets he could not be happy. But on the great, wide ocean, he would find peace.

Michael began to wave enthusiastically. The weather vane moved from side to side, dangerously. He took no notice. He shouted to the far-away vessel. Nobody could hear him, of course.

# CHAPTER FOUR

## *THE STEEPLECHASE*

Down below, sailor Jan Evertsz was on his way home. He felt happy to be in port again after a long voyage. It was good to see the familiar homes again. Flushing has a beautiful church and an impressive tower, too, he thought. Evertsz stopped to take a good look at it. But wait a minute, was there somebody still working at the very top of the tower?

A muscular carpenter, cutting some wood at the base of the tower was looking at Evertsz. "What's the trouble, sailor?" he asked. "You look as if you have never seen our church before."

"I've seen our church often enough, but I've never seen a church that uses a man for a weather vane."

"What are you talking about?" the big man asked as he followed the sailor's gaze upwards. "Well, I'll say . . . but that isn't a man, it's a boy. What's he doing up there?"

The sailor shook his head. "You're right. It's a boy alright. But he'll never come down alive. The spire is as slippery as an eel."

The carpenter agreed. "I think we better get the sheriff and his men to take him down." Without waiting for Jan to answer, he left.

Meanwhile, quite a crowd had gathered to see what was going on. The people pointed at the top of the tower where Michael continued to imagine himself sailing to far away countries. Then he noticed the people below him. At first he didn't understand what they were doing there and why they were all looking up. Were they waving at him? If they thought that he had found a great observation spot, he would have to agree with them.

Then again, they didn't *really* seem to be waving at all. They wouldn't be thinking that he was in danger, would they? As far as he was concerned, there was no danger at all.

Then he noticed the sheriff and his men coming. They even carried some ladders! They would get him down, Michael realized. And if those men got hold of him, he wouldn't be happy for a long time. Better get down quickly!

But getting down was easier said than done, Michael found out. The spire's slick shingles offered no handhold, and he certainly couldn't get a firm foothold. While he kept his arms firmly around the pole of the weather vane, he felt around with his feet, uselessly. He didn't panic. Instead, he broke one of the limestone shingles with a kick of his heel and stuck his foot in the opening. It held. Minutes later he was at the top platform again. He looked down to see what was going on. Below him, the sheriff's men were climbing the ladders! Now Michael had to act quickly. He flung his arms around one of the poles and slid down to the next platform. His pursuers had arrived at the next level down.

"Come here, you!" one of them shouted. But Michael knew better than to answer. No Sir, he would not go down to meet them. They better come up to get him if they could.

The men intended to do just that. They put their ladder against the scaffold and began to climb.

Michael had been waiting for this. Just when the men were halfway between the two platforms, Michael swung his arms around the next pole and slid down, bypassing the furious lawmen.

Seconds later he landed hard on the street, sprang up, and disappeared around the corner of the church before the crowd realized what had happened.

Two blocks away from the church he stopped to catch his breath.

# CHAPTER FIVE

## *SAILING?*

When Michael came home late that afternoon, he was surprised to find his mother alone in the kitchen.

"Good afternoon," he said, casually. "Where's Father?"

His mother stopped her work for a minute and looked at her boy. "Father is visiting somebody. It's about you, Michael. Your teacher was here this afternoon. He said that you haven't done what you had promised this morning. And the sheriff has been here as well. Michael, how did you *dare* to climb to the top of the tower? Don't you ever see any danger? Father is really angry. He . . ."

Suddenly Mother stopped her outburst. Michael still stood in the door opening with his hand still on the door knob. His head was bent.

"Michael?" Mother said gently.

He didn't answer but closed the door, passed by his mother, and climbed the ladder to the loft. There he fell on his bed and buried his head in the pillow.

He didn't cry, but he could not think either. Nobody seemed to understand him, not even his own mother. Nobody knew how much he loved the sea. Mother didn't know it and Father didn't understand it. And Father should have understood, since he had been at sea. Why didn't his parents allow him to make just one ocean voyage so that he could find out for himself?

Michael rolled on his back and folded his hands behind his head. He stared through the semi-darkness at the little window. A strange emptiness came upon him and somehow he felt that being all by himself at this time was the best.

About an hour later he heard his father enter the kitchen. Michael could hear voices, but since his father was keeping his voice down, Michael couldn't understand what was being said. His mother's remarks were short. It seemed that she was asking some questions. Michael lifted his head off the pillow to hear better. It didn't help much. The only thing he could make out was that his father's voice sounded quiet. His anger had obviously settled. Michael felt relieved. His father was really a very kind man, but when he became angry, he often had difficulty controlling himself.

"Come down, Michael!" his father suddenly boomed. It frightened Michael a bit. He would rather go to sleep without his supper than to face his father at this moment.

When he came downstairs, Michael realized that something else was waiting for him. Both parents sat at the table. As usual, his mother was doing some mending. His father seemed quiet as if he were reflecting on something.

"Michael," he began, "this day was a bad one for you. I was furious with you when I heard the complaints from both the schoolmaster and the sheriff. Confronting you then would have been a bad thing. Do you understand that?"

Michael merely shook his head in the affirmative.

His father continued. "I left the house and visited a friend. I told him everything. He really is a wise man and he spoke to me for a long time. He suggested that we take you out of school. Your mother and I agree. It seems to be the only logical solution to your problems."

Michael couldn't believe it. He was going to sea! His eyes widened and he was about to jump up and give his father a hug when he was cut short. "Now don't get too excited yet. You know that we don't want you to go to sea, mostly because we think that you are still too young. So I visited someone else and found a job for you that has a lot to do with ships. It will be good for you and in our family we can most certainly use another income. The person I spoke to was Seigneur Lampsens. He seems to like you and he is willing to take you on as a helper in his ropery. You will be making all kinds of ropes for his ships. We agreed that you start tomorrow. Your mother and I hope that this will be the best solution. We can talk about sailing at some point in the future, perhaps. What do you think?"

Michael had to consider this new development for a moment. He didn't know what to answer. "Maybe I'll like it better than school," he replied. But he had no idea what the inside of a ropery looked like and the thought of working there didn't excite him. Then again, it had to be better than school. Anything was better than school.

"That's it, then," Adrian Michielszoon continued. "Have some supper and then go to sleep at once. Tomorrow you'll get up the same time I do. We'll leave the house together."

"Yes, Father," Michael replied slowly, thinking how he would have to get up at four o'clock in the morning every day of the week except on Sundays. He wouldn't get home until after five and there would be no time to play. Although he was just ten years old he had to live the life of a grown man. He would have to work long hours without rest, the same as other workers did. Yet there was a bright side to it. No more school for him.

The next morning Michael, bleary eyed, ate his breakfast with his father. Mother had been up to do a few things, but she had gone to bed again for it was still early and there wasn't all that much she could do. The other children were still sleeping.

A few minutes later Michael and his father left the house. They didn't speak much. Their footsteps reverberated off the houses and cobblestones. It was still dark out. Here and there a little light glimmered behind a window.

At the corner of the street they parted. "Do your best, Michael," his father said.

"Yes, I will," was his promise.

* * *

The work in the ropery was not what Michael had expected. In fact, in some ways it was a lot like school. Maybe worse.

# CHAPTER SIX

## *ROPE WORK*

In an almost dark, wooden shed stood the twining machine. A large oaken wheel fed the twine to old Frank Lieven, who made it into rope. It was Michael's job to turn that big wheel. At first he turned it too slowly, causing the old man to grumble. "A little faster, slowpoke. My fingers are getting bored." So Michael sped it up a bit. Now Lieven grumbled again. "Not so fast, you good-for-nothing little rascal. I'm not twenty anymore!"

Michael shrugged Lieven's complaints off. The job was dull. There was just one little window in the shop and if he stood on his toes, he could look through the half-dirty glass and see some mast tops of ships in port. The old man didn't talk very much and Michael didn't feel like conversing, either. That made the time creep along. Minutes blurred into terribly monotonous hours.

What bothered Michael the most was that the shop had four high walls, little fresh air, and no promise of adventure — just like school. He had promised to do his best, though, and this time he would make sure that he was just as good as his word. When he was at home he didn't complain about the four walls and grumpy old Lieven and he didn't mention that he wanted to see ships. At the end of the first week he proudly handed his first-earned wages to his mother. Six shiny nickels. Thirty cents, less than a penny for each hour he had worked.

During the second week, however, things began to go wrong. Michael didn't know what to do with himself when Lieven had to put another huge ball of twine on the machine and splice it into strands before he could resume the turning of the wheel. At first, Michael just watched the old man, but after a day or two, he didn't quite know what to do with himself. On the third day he decided to step outside for a minute while Lieven put the twine on the machine.

"Where are you going, Boy?" grumbled Lieven.

"Getting some fresh air, Sir," was Michael's reply.

The old man mumbled something, but Michael didn't hear what he said. He closed the door behind him, put his hands into his pockets and leaned against the doorpost. The fresh air did him some good. A few minutes later old Lieven called him back to work. No problem whatsoever.

The very next day didn't go as well. When he stood outside again, leaning against the window sill, Michael noticed three mast tops moving slowly behind the roofs of the homes in front of him. That made him forget the ropewalk, his duty, and his pay. Within minutes he was at the docks to witness the arrival of a ship from the East. By the time he remembered that he had work to do, it was too late to go back. He just went home and said nothing about what had happened.

The next morning Lieven scolded him and he got a reprimand from Seigneur Lampsens. Michael felt ashamed of himself and promised that it would not happen again. Yet only a few hours later his feet carried him to the harbour once more. Somehow it seemed that there was a power stronger than he was; a magnet that practically pulled him to where the ships were anchored.

That afternoon Seigneur Lampsens sent for Michael's father.

"Listen, Adrian," he said, "why don't you let your boy make just one trip on a merchant vessel? It may take the restlessness out of him. And if not, he should probably become a sailor for good. As it stands now, he's useless. I pay him to work, not to run away."

Adrian Michielszoon just stood there, squeezing and folding between his thick, calloused fingers the cap he had taken off before entering Seigneur Lampsens' office. "Maybe you're right, Sir. Maybe we should just try it."

"You know," Seigneur Lampsens continued, "your boy is as strong as a lion and he is honest. But there's just no way I can keep him under the ropewalk's roof. We both know that he'll likely make a fine sailor, but you have to let him go. If you want me to, I'll find a good ship's father for him on one of my vessels. Let him make a few short runs to England, just to get some experience. You never know, he might get seasick and never want to sail again! What do you think?"

Adrian sighed. "I think you're right. I am very happy with your offer and I know that my son didn't deserve it. Thank you very much."

That evening his father told Michael about the decision, and Michael ran around in the small house whooping and bounding.

His mother just smiled, but in his enthusiasm Michael didn't notice that she had tears in her eyes.

So it was that on the day after Christmas, in the year of our Lord, 1618, Michael Adrianszoon and his mother walked to the harbour where the ship was moored. It would be Michael's new home for the following months. On Christmas day Mother and Michael had packed an old wooden box with the necessities that she could spare. Last of all she put a Bible into it. She had caressed the book with her hands. "Your Bible, Michael," she had said to him, "I trust that you will read it every day."

"Of course I will, Mother. You know I will."

The two approached the ship in silence. It was one of Seigneur Lampsens' vessels bound for Italy with a smelly load of fish in its holds. It was not a man-o-war or even especially pretty, but in Michael's eyes it was the largest and most beautiful vessel he had ever seen.

The closer they came to the ship, the longer Michael's strides became. He felt grown-up now although he had just become eleven years old. He was hired to be the boatswain's mate's helper and he knew that it involved many unfamiliar responsibilities.

At the gangplank, his mother stopped. Michael put his box down and put his arms around her. "Goodbye, Mother," he said. He had wanted his voice to sound grown-up and mature, but somehow there was a frog in it and his goodbye had sounded a bit hoarse.

"Goodbye, Michael. I'll pray for you every day. I know that there are many rough men on your ship. I don't want you to grow up like them."

"I know, Mother. You don't have to worry. I won't be like them. I want to become a captain, a good captain."

His mother smiled. Whenever she did that, Michael knew that she had the most beautiful smile in the whole world.

He picked up his box and put it under his arm.

"Goodbye, Mother."

And with that he walked on board. Behind him, he left his mother and the only world he knew as he stepped into this new world of rigging and planking, men and cargo. He didn't look behind him. Instead, he listened to the ships creaking timbers and watched the deck move slowly from side to side. Even in port there was a slight rocking motion. This would take some getting used to, he thought. At length, he was greeted by an old man with a face as wrinkled as crumpled paper. This was a man who had spent years at sea.

"So you're the little boy who got thrown out of school and got fired at Seigneur's ropewalk. And now you want to become a sailor, eh? You'd better watch your step every inch of the way. I'll be there to make sure that you become a sailor, and if not, I'll throw you to the sharks single-handedly. Get that?" By this time the old deck-hand was inches away from Michael's face.

"Y-yes, Sir," he stammered lamely.

"That's good. I'll be your ship's father for this trip. And by the way, my name is Jos. But you call me 'Sir.' Understand?"

"Yes, Sir," Michael answered and over his shoulder he looked at his mother, who must have heard every word old Jos had said.

"You can wait here and wave to your mother until we're out of port. Then I'll show you your quarters and then the fun will begin." Jos' voice was still the same, but if Michael hadn't been so frightened, he might have detected a bit of tenderness in it.

Michael later discovered that Jos had sent his own boy to sea on what was supposed to have been a safe trip, but the boy had not returned to port. Neither had the vessel.

Michael put his arms on the railing. The commands for departure had already been given. He waved at his mother. She smiled at him again.

Within minutes, as the distance between him and his mother became greater, she became smaller and smaller until he could not see her anymore. It occurred to him that he was where he had imagined himself as he sat on the church roof that one day. His father had said that far from home the Lord's eyes would never lose sight of him and that the Lord would keep him safe. Those were words that Michael would never forget.

"Did you lose your mother, Michael?" a voice behind him taunted. He wheeled around and found himself eye to eye with his old buddy Jan Company. The two had played together on the streets of Flushing, had gone fishing together on the dike, and to the catechism classes that were held in the big church. They were best friends. Brothers almost, but they certainly didn't look much like one another. Jan was black. He had been adopted in Africa by a Dutch sailor.

"Jan, what are you doing here?" Michael stammered.

Jan just grinned and whenever he did that he showed his beautiful white teeth. Michael was missing some himself. Too many fights. "Same as you, Michael. I'm a sailor now."

Michael was overjoyed to have a friend on board. But old Jos, although he showed no mercy and continued to be tough with him, proved to be friendly, in the end.

The captain, who had been informed about Michael's problems, was pleasantly surprised when he noticed how the hard-to-handle boy of Adrian Michielszoon became a hard-working, obedient young sailor who made even old Jos proud.

In his whole life, Michael had never been so happy. Every day he practically drank in the salt air. The waves' steady lapping against the ship's hull was like music to him and he even came to appreciate the ship's chores. He climbed the masts (which was scary at first because of how far they swayed) and mopped the deck and lashed the ropes with the best of humour.

No doubt about it. This was the life.

# CHAPTER SEVEN

## *SOLDIER AND PRISONER*

Long before Michael was born, the Dutch people were engaged in a war against the king of Spain. This terrible conflict lasted eighty years. It had begun because the king of Spain had raised taxes[2] and persecuted the Protestants — the followers of Martin Luther and John Calvin.

The Eighty Years' War began in the year 1568, but when Michael was only a baby, the warring parties agreed to a twelve year truce. As Michael grew up, his country remained at peace. Yet when he was old enough to go to sea, people were talking about the possibility that the war would be resumed.

In 1621 Dutchmen were called once more to defend their country and to throw off the yoke of the Spaniards.

Michael was just fourteen years old when he returned from another journey. He was a seasoned sailor now and many captains would have loved to have him as a crew member. Michael, though, had other plans.

"Mother," he had said, "I am going to join Prince Maurice's troops and fight for the house of Orange."

His mother had looked up, surprised. "But Michael, you're only fourteen years old! Fighting a war is a man's job, it's not for young boys like you."

"But I have to. The Prince needs every able-bodied man to defend our land. You know how cruel the Spaniards are! I just have to go. All the other sailors are talking about it!"

---

[2] The King of Spain had been lord of the Netherlands. In a manner similar to his predecessors, Philip II had promised to maintain privileges which had been granted to many cities and towns. By raising certain taxes the Spanish king broke these promises.

And that had been the end of the discussion. Although his parents were opposed to his decision, Michael said farewell to his captain and the crew and set out to the place where the Prince's troops were stationed.

Two days later he reported to an officer.

"Your name, young man?"

"Michael De Ruyter, Sir," he said, proudly. "My grandfather was a horseman in the army. That's how we got the family name of De Ruyter."

"Interesting." The officer snorted. "And what might be your trade? Horseman, maybe?"

"No, Sir, I've been a sailor for three years."

Michael looked straight into the officer's blue eyes hoping that the man would not ask him his age. When the recruiter only jerked his head in the direction of another officer, Michael was relieved. Maybe it was because Prince Maurice needed every man he could get, he reasoned, even if the man was only a boy of not quite fifteen years of age.

It wasn't long before Michael marched into Germany as a foot soldier in the Prince's army. The Spaniards had captured the city of Goch. The Prince hoped to confront the enemy and was sure that he could be victorious in a battle with the Spanish general Spinola. The Spaniard, though, didn't want to meet the Prince's army. While Prince Maurice moved his troops eastward, Spinola went in a westerly direction and prepared to attack the Dutch city of Bergen op Zoom.

After Dutch scouts had reported the Spaniards' position to the Prince, Maurice sent his swift cavalry to help the besieged soldiers.

Having bought a horse with the money he had saved while at sea, the young sailor turned soldier was also assigned a place in the cavalry. Making use of the darkness of a cloudy night, this section of the army boarded a boat, crossed the river, and entered the city of Bergen op Zoom without being seen.

The next morning an officer ordered Michael to take his position on top of the city wall. Someone gave him a musket, but the weapon was much too awkward and heavy for a boy his age so they gave him a flintlock pistol instead. Just the same, the officers were pleased with the young soldier and when it was time for the troops to be paid, Michael received the same wages as any older man — twelve guilders for a month's service. Far more than he had earned making ropes, that was for sure.

One evening an officer asked for a few dozen volunteers for a stealthy midnight attack on the Spaniards. They hoped the enemy would be soundly asleep in their tents. The raid would destroy as much of the Spaniards' belongings and supplies as possible. The raiders would then retreat quickly behind the safety of the city walls. To the surprise of many of the men, Michael volunteered.

Shortly after midnight the city gates were flung open and the Dutch raced out like wild men into the enemy camp. They had their horses gallop among the tents. They ripped open or overturned the tents, loaded food supplies and weapons, and charged back into the city before the Spanish could even react.

Michael thought that the whole thing was terrifying, but strangely also fun. The raid had a purpose. Because of it, the Spaniards learned to respect the daring Dutchmen and became afraid of meeting them on a battlefield. Even General Spinola wasn't certain that he could defeat Prince Maurice easily. Eleven weeks later the Spaniards broke camp and disappeared.

* * *

Winter was approaching. This meant that there would not be much activity. The Prince ordered his troops to settle down in their winter camps, and Michael asked for permission to go home. He had better things to do and knew that there would be a ship waiting for him.

Two days later he left for Flushing where his parents welcomed him joyfully. Soon he began to look for a ship to return to the life he had learned to love. He didn't have to look very long. The war with Spain was still raging and the Dutch needed sailors to man the warships that had to protect merchant vessels against enemy attack.

His mother didn't like seeing Michael leave again. The night before he departed again, she spoke to him, crying just a little. "I don't want to lose you, Michael. War is so terrible. Why don't you find a job in town?"

"I know, Mother, what war is like. But I'm not cut out to stay on shore. I'm only happy on board a ship. You of all people should know that."

His father agreed. He realized that there was no use trying to persuade his son to stay on land. "God go with you, Son. Mother and I will always pray for you."

Michael nodded. "Thank you, Father. And I will always pray for both of you, I promise."

This was the second promise that Michael was able to keep. He had not stopped reading his Bible. By now it was dog-eared and battered.

When Michael left Flushing, the captain gave him a promotion. He was no longer the lowest paid man on the ship. He decided that he would prove to his parents and shipmates that he deserved every cent.

The ship sailed safely through the Strait of Dover without spotting Spanish warships. Yet, when the vessel entered the treacherous Bay of Biscay, a Spanish warship was sighted. The captain immediately shouted his orders for the attack. Within minutes the vessel changed course and headed straight for the Spaniard. Moments later the cannons began to fire.

As the ships came closer to each other, the captain ordered, "Prepare to board!"

Michael stood with many other sailors at the railing, ready to jump over to the enemy vessel. His heart pounded in his throat. Never before in his young life had he faced hand to hand combat at such close quarters. "Lord, help me!" he prayed furtively. He was just a boy and the Spaniards looked tall and menacing.

When the command was given, sailors used grapplers, long poles with steel hooks, to pull the ships against each other. Michael was the first to jump, followed by his comrades. However, as he landed on the Spanish vessel, he tripped and fell flat on the deck. An enemy sailor immediately stabbed at his face cutting deep into his cheek. Michael tried to scream above the noise of the battle as blood streamed down his face, sticky and warm. The Spaniard was ready to stab him again. Just then, one of Michael's comrades was beside him, fighting back the enemy. His life was saved.

Strong arms carried him back to his own ship where the doctor cleaned his face with whisky, which made it hurt worse. The wound was closed with a dirty ship's needle and thread. No anesthetic. No sterile equipment.

By the time his face was stitched together, the battle was over. The Spaniards surrendered and were driven together on the main deck. The poor men fully expected to be thrown overboard and drowned, but the Dutch captain showed mercy. He ordered them locked up in the hold and gave orders to sink the enemy ship. Michael remembered the tactic.

He sat on deck, and felt the bandages on his face with his stubby fingers. The pain was searing, but he managed to smile again.

* * *

For the next few days no enemy ships were sighted. The crew had a chance to repair some of the damage the ship had sustained during the battle, but fear gripped the hearts of the men when, from nowhere, four Spanish warships came closing in on the Dutch vessel as if they had materialized from the water itself. Michael felt his pulse quicken and his throat constrict; a panicky sensation that was becoming all

too familiar. The Dutch didn't stand a chance against so many! "What now, Lord?" he asked. He didn't want his life to end here, so far from home.

Michael could not serve on deck since his wounds had not healed and the boatswain ordered him down below to guard the prisoners. A terrible battle started above him. First the cannons boomed and then Michael could feel his ship being bumped by two Spanish ships, one on each side. From the commotion he learned that Spaniards had come on board. Suddenly it became quiet. The Dutch captain had surrendered.

Now the roles were reversed. The Spaniards that Michael had guarded were now guarding the Dutch sailors. Michael and his friends were crowded together and feared the worst. But, probably because the Dutch had spared them, the Spaniards didn't kill them. Instead they planned to take them ashore and dispatch them as slaves on huge Spanish galleons. There, they would be chained to seats and ordered to row endlessly until they died from exhaustion and mistreatment.

* * *

There was no port on the coast they now approached. The Spaniards sailed their vessels until they became stuck on the beach. Then they ordered the prisoners to be pushed overboard and forced them to wade to the shore.

Michael stood neck-deep in the water with two of his shipmates.

"Let's make an awful racket and confuse the Spicks,"[3] one suggested. "Maybe we can make a run for it."

The others nodded. It was better to try and hopefully make it to safety than it was to do as the Spaniards said.

As soon as the water was shallow enough to allow them to move quickly, men began hollering and Michael and his two friends ran. At first a few Spaniards began to run after them, but their water-logged boots slowed them down. They couldn't use their muskets either since they had left them on the deck of their ship for fear that they would get wet when they jumped overboard.

---

[3] A derogatory name for Spaniards.

Michael and his friends ran and ran until they reached the shelter of an outcropping of rocks. When they finally looked back, they saw that the Spaniards had stopped pursuing them.

After having rested for some time, the three began their long walk home. They made their way along the beaches until they reached southern France. They had to beg for their food and experienced God's care over them.

The walk through France to the shores of their homeland took a very long time. The clothes of the three boys were torn, their bodies dirty, and they lost weight.

So it was that three miserable-looking, exhausted young men finally found their way back to the city of Flushing.

When Michael stood in front of his mother later that day, she didn't recognize him. His hair was long and matted. His clothes were shabby and covered in mud. He smelled. He had grown a beard. It wasn't until he embraced her and muttered, simply, "I'm home" that she knew that her son had returned.

# CHAPTER EIGHT

## *ADULTHOOD*

Michael needed to regain his strength. It took several weeks. His mother hoped that her son had had his fill of warfare and adventures and prayed that he would stay home, but Michael had other plans. He made daily visits to the harbour and even to the office of Seigneur Lampsens. Naturally, Seigneur Lampsens was happy to have Michael back. He suspected that the young De Ruyter had a bright future.

Michael had mixed feelings when he learned that Seigneur Lampsens thought so highly of him. He was displeased with himself. In order to get somewhere in life, a person needed an education. With the little education he had he would never be able to become an officer on a ship and neither would he be able to provide for a family. If he ever found anyone to marry, he would just be dragging her into a life of constant financial hardships. Michael didn't want to do that.

Even before he went back to Seigneur Lampsens for a job, he went to see his old teacher.

"Sir, I made a big mistake when I was in your class. I should have stayed in school and I should have worked harder. I'm almost twenty years old now and it's too late to go back." Michael crunched and twisted his hat in his hands.

The old teacher smiled. He was much smaller and thinner than Michael remembered. "I remember you too well, Michael." There was a mischievous twinkle in the teacher's eyes. "But no, it is not too late. It's never too late. You can't go back to the classroom, but you can come to me as often as you wish and I will help you make up for all the time lost.

But Michael, I'll only teach you if you promise to stick with it."

Michael promised. That same evening he started the difficult job of catching up to those who had stayed in school much longer than he had.

It was difficult. Hands that were used to ropes and beams fumbled awkwardly with the dainty quill and inkwell. Although he could count and read, he was behind in mathematics and spelling. All the same, he spent a great deal of time with his books, and actually began to enjoy them.

In the meantime, Michael recovered from his battlefield wounds and was rehired by Seigneur Lampsens. For the next few years he served on various ships and made trips around England and the Mediterranean Sea. There were no frightening experiences and no battles to be fought on these journeys, which was fine with him. At the end of each trip he stashed his earnings and spent very little of it on luxuries. Other sailors drank or gambled their money away, but Michael saved every penny he could.

He was no typical sailor. He would go to church when he was in port and then he would put a generous gift in the collection box as his father had taught him. The money he had stashed away would grow, one guilder at a time, until he had enough to purchase his own ship. That was his dream.

During the stormy winter months ships stayed in port. Michael used this spare time to continue his studies. When the old teacher informed him that he had taught Michael all he knew, Michael shook his hand vigorously. "Thank you so much, Sir, for helping me along. You know, when I was a boy I didn't spend enough time in the school to see how fine a teacher you were. Now I know. Are you sure we're done?"

The old man laughed. "Oh, *we're* done, alright, but you're not! Learning takes a lifetime, Michael. The time has come for you to study navigation, ship building, and languages, which, quite frankly, I do not know much about. I suggest that you find a retired sea captain to guide you further."

The very next day Michael found just the person he was looking for. The old sailor was living quite nearby. His name was Captain Vis, a tall, reedy man whose gait was perpetually tipped sideways from years spent at sea. Just as Michael had spent hours with his former teacher, he now spent numerous hours with Vis, sitting by the window of the captain's stately home, tinkering with maps and compasses and charts of the night sky.

Seigneur Lampsens was excited by the development of his young friend. Michael had been asking Lampsens all kinds of questions, some of which had stumped the old nobleman. Furthermore, Lampsens noticed that Michael possessed an uncanny trading sense. The company could certainly use the services of a sailor who was also a keen businessman. So it happened that Seigneur Lampsens gave Michael a number of promotions within his company, until he finally appointed him to the position of navigator.

There were other developments in the life of the young sailor, but none was more important than Michael's development as a strong Christian. Although he still had to struggle with his temper, (especially when he noticed the laziness or incompetence of certain sailors), he was honest and just. He knew that his life was in the hands of his heavenly Father, even though life was often difficult and merciless.

And then there was Maria. Michael had known her casually for a number of years. He occasionally took her out for long walks around the city and the harbour. They talked for hours about ships and sails and joked about the way that old Reverend De Korte's eyes fluttered when he preached.

Once they were walking on a particularly cold day. The clouds were rolling in from the North Sea and darkening up the sky. "You know, Maria," Michael had said, "I think you and I should get married." It wasn't quite what he had wanted to say, or how he had wanted to say it, but he hoped Maria knew what his heart meant.

Maria, who had been expecting something like this, pulled him close to her, and as the first drops of rain began to drop full and heavy to the ground she replied, "I love you, too, Michael."

The wedding took place after a year of preparations and discussions between the families. Michael and Maria moved into a pretty little home with large windows that would let in the sunlight from over the harbour where they had taken their walks. Michael was twenty-four years old now, a burly and fiercely-handsome young man. His hands were large and strong like his father's had been, and had been tempered by the lashing of winds and rain. His dark brown eyes were warm and forgiving but quick to whip up into a maelstrom when he was provoked.

Within a year, Maria was expecting their first child, and De Ruyter made a room ready for the baby. They both worked hard at decorating it. When De Ruyter was at sea, Maria would sew and knit baby clothes and blankets, softly humming hymns or little ditties she would make up on the spur of the moment.

Things seemed to be going fabulously. De Ruyter had received another promotion and was now the first officer on his ship, he had married the most wonderful girl in the world, and together they were looking forward to the joy of parenthood.

It all stopped the day Maria gave birth to a baby girl. Something went wrong. The midwife had called in a doctor to help, but he could do nothing. Immediately following the birth of the baby, Maria died. Three weeks later the baby that De Ruyter had named Alida after his grandmother died as well.

It was something Michael could not understand. Why did the Lord give him so much only to wrest it all away from him again? He read passages from the book of Job, from the gospel of Matthew, but nothing seemed to bring him much comfort. It was his former teacher who provided De Ruyter with an analogy he could understand.

"The Lord does not spare sorrow even from those who love Him with their whole heart," he had said. "Sometimes He uses sadness to bind us closer to Him. When a storm hits, drop your sails, secure the tiller arm, and trust God to carry you through. That kind of devotion is what God requires of His servants."

A few days later he returned to his ship to continue the life he had loved, in the hope that he would overcome his sorrow.

The first few trips were very different from any he had ever undertaken and helped to keep his mind from drifting toward Maria and Alida. His ship, *The Green Lion*, was not sent out to carry freight like his previous ships were. *The Green Lion* was fitted out to go on the whale hunt near Greenland. Life on board was quite different again from what he was accustomed to. Instead of looking out for pirates or enemy vessels, the men on board kept their eyes peeled for the big mammals. Yet there was something about it all that didn't please De Ruyter. In a way he felt sorry for the whales who fought so gallantly for their own lives only to be hauled in and hacked to pieces.

In his second year as a whale hunter, things changed dramatically. Instead of sailing north, his ship's whaling fleet sailed all the way to the southern tip of South America. Although it turned out to be a dangerous journey, a number of events during it served to convince his fellow sailors that De Ruyter was one of the best navigators of the world.

As the ships approached Cape Horn, one of the storms that the area is famous for broke loose. The wind pushed and bullied the vessels into masses of ice, calling on the utmost of the skills of the navigators to prevent the ships from being bashed into driftwood. One ship became stuck between two icebergs and was crushed. Other ships ran into invisible ice formations and sank. Only the ship that had De Ruyter as its navigator managed to avoid disaster.[4] By God's aid, De Ruyter's instinct and sharp commands had saved the vessel. A day later it sailed into an open bay where it waited until the storm had blown itself out.

The next few days were used to take on board sailors whose ships had been destroyed and to make the necessary repairs to the rigging. Just when the skipper felt that the journey could be continued, a new storm broke loose. This time fierce winds thundered in from the mainland with such destructive power that the anchor chains broke and De Ruyter's ship

was blown out of the bay into the sea. The icebergs were still lying in wait and there was fear in the hearts of all the men. De Ruyter used all his knowledge and skill to prevent the vessel from being crushed in between the ice floes. Suddenly the tension broke and the young navigator let out a deep sigh and thanked the Lord as he saw open waters ahead of him.

---

[4] One time his was the only one of twenty-six ships that survived a storm; another time his was the only one of sixteen; and once his was the only one of six to survive.

The danger was seemingly past, but the wind changed in a new direction, extending a claw of cold weather ahead of itself. The temperature plummeted, freezing the sails. The men tried fervidly to lower whatever sails they could reach, but it was useless. De Ruyter watched helplessly as even the small sails were ripped to brittle shreds. He now had the almost impossible task of navigating a vessel without the help of its sails. The wind changed direction once more, blowing the ship back to where it had come from. De Ruyter stayed on deck in spite of the extreme cold and battled with the wind and his own tiredness, having been on his feet for three days without rest.

A day later the wind had again gone to sleep. Once more in the safety of the bay the crew repaired the sails by sewing together the torn pieces. Other men were sent to shore for supplies and, taking advantage of the storm's exhaustion, the ship tentatively went on its return journey.

De Ruyter used the first days to catch up on his own sleep. Yet he also took time to speak to the Lord and to thank Him for the safety that He had provided. The captain and his men praised De Ruyter for his skills, but De Ruyter knew better. Certainly, the Lord had provided him with great skills, but the whole matter of the safety of the ship and its crew was the work of his loving Father. "Don't thank me," he had mumbled. "I'm only an instrument. It's the Lord Who shielded us."

De Ruyter had remembered his teacher's words. Drop the sails. Lash the tiller arm. Trust God to take care of you.

* * *

When the ship limped into port a few weeks later, her sails a patchwork quilt of tattered rags, De Ruyter went home.

He had avoided his house. The furniture was damp and dusty. There were no flowers on the table. There was nobody to welcome him, nobody humming and scuttling around the sitting room. Only the quiet and the damp.

De Ruyter eased into the chair by the window. Particles of dust caught the rays of sunlight that were streaming into the house from over the ocean. He tightened his grip on the armrests and stared out at the harbour, watching the ships come and go. At sea there was noise: the pulse of water under the prow of the ship, the creak of water-sodden beams and the hoarse shouts of men in the rigging.

But nothing was louder than this.

Occasionally he would go out for a stroll. Winter was approaching and it would be months before he could sail again. Weeks and weeks of loneliness and boredom lay ahead. When he sat at home he could almost feel the tides moving in and out of the harbour. It was as if he had the salt water in his blood. "You should get married again, De Ruyter," his friends advised him. Every time they said this, he would wave them off. He simply didn't want to forget Maria, and it seemed to him that there was nobody who could take her place. Privately, he convinced himself that he needed no one; nothing but a ship and the salty kisses of the sea.

That was, until the day he met Cornelia Engels. Cornelia was a demure girl whose eyes rested gently on the big sailor. She understood his sorrow and his loneliness. He sensed that she was the one to give him the happiness and the security he had lost. De Ruyter noticed the sincerity of the young lady and was touched by her soft voice and her loving interest in him. She was like Maria, but different too. The way she angled her head while she was listening, the way her fingers smoothed out the wrinkles on her dress when she sat, her almost embarrassed little laugh. All of these were different from Maria.

De Ruyter made his decision quickly. He would be at sea again soon. He asked Cornelia to marry him. Her reply, he could see, was heartfelt.

"I would love to, Michael."

God had seen him through this storm, too.

# CHAPTER NINE

## *THE PIRATES AT DUNKIRK*

Dunkirk is a town in northern France, close to the Belgian border. It is situated at the Strait of Dover and, when you stand at the harbour of Dunkirk on a clear day, you can see the English coast.

During the seventeenth century, Dunkirk was a brooding nest teeming with pirates — bloodthirsty, ruthless sailors. They were thieves and misfits. Pirates belonged to no particular country. They seized ships, sold the cargo and imprisoned or enslaved the crews.

De Ruyter knew all about pirates. Many of his fellow sailors had had the misfortune of meeting up with these seaborne thieves and had been killed. Others were sold to enemy navies to spend the rest of their days wallowing behind the oars of clumsy galleons.

Shortly after De Ruyter had married Cornelia Engels, he received word from Seigneur Lampsens that he was to command a ship with orders to search, find, and destroy as many of the Dunkirk pirates as possible. Seigneur Lampsens explained the mission to De Ruyter.

"Did you know, De Ruyter, that those pirates have taken more than two hundred fishing boats from the port of Maassluis alone within six years? Do you know how many of my cargo ships they have taken during the same period? Any idea how many of our fine men lost their lives because of them?" Old Lampsens body shook most of the time, but this time he was shaking with rage.

De Ruyter stood up from his chair and said, "I know, Seigneur. I have kept track of them. I'll accept your commission and I'll teach these pirates that the Dutch aren't cowards."

A few days later De Ruyter's privateer[5] left Flushing. He was disappointed with the crew. They were, he thought, a group of scoundrels barely better than the pirates themselves. De Ruyter knew that a ship is only as good as its men. All the same, it was his first real chance to command a vessel. That in itself was thrilling.

As De Ruyter and his crew of misfits sailed through the English channel, they sighted two pirate ships. They were easy enough to recognize, for they almost always flew the pirates' flag, the dreaded "Jolly Roger."

Although it was to be two against one, De Ruyter ordered his crew to prepare for the attack. He heard grumbling from the men on deck, but one look at Captain De Ruyter told them that he was serious indeed. His jaw was squarely set and his eyes were focused on the two ships ahead. The crew obeyed his commands, though reluctantly.

He first attacked the pirate ship closest to him with daring and calculated cannon fire. During the battle, De Ruyter leapt about fiercely, barking orders in a loud voice that was hard as iron. His ship caused so much damage that the pirate captain ordered his flag to be lowered in surrender. De Ruyter ordered his helmsman to steer straight for the second pirate. This one decided to flee, but his ship was much slower than De Ruyter's. The captain of the second pirate vessel surrendered without firing a shot.

De Ruyter boarded the captured ships personally and saw to it that the crews were tied up and put into the holds. Then

---

[5] A privateer was an armed ship owned by a private person (like Lampsens) holding a government licence to attack enemy ships. Pirates, on the other hand, worked for themselves only.

he ordered the captured vessels to be hooked to a tow line and taken to Flushing.

This time, though, the crew became visibly upset. They protested loudly. "You can't do this," they protested. "It's too dangerous!" Even the officers refused to obey. Finally De Ruyter had to order the captured crew transferred to the hold of his own ship. He had the captured vessels sunk by cannon fire.

When the two ships were reduced to burning husks, De Ruyter ordered the crew to keep on searching for more Dunkirk pirates. Again they refused. The men knew that they had earned a large reward for the work already done and were eager to go home. De Ruyter began to think that he didn't want the command of a warship again if crews of those vessels were anything like this bunch. He sailed back to Flushing and explained to Seigneur Lampsens that he would not command another privateer again unless he could select his own crew.

Seigneur Lampsens understood, but he couldn't provide the kind of crew that his captain wanted. Instead, Lampsens offered him the command of a large merchant vessel that would soon be ready to leave for a journey to Brazil.

Of course Seigneur Lampsens didn't forget to thank De Ruyter for his services on board the warship and paid him a share of the booty — a handsome amount of money.

A few days later, after having said goodbye to his wife again, De Ruyter boarded his new ship and departed. Once out in open sea, he handed his command to the first officer and retreated to his cabin. When the first officer entered an hour later, he was surprised to see his captain scribbling away on some paper in the light of his cabin window.

"May I ask what you are doing, Sir?" he asked politely.

De Ruyter smiled and turned the sheets around so that his officer could see them. "I am working on a new way of conducting war at sea," he replied. "The way in which sea battles are executed is no longer of any value. It lacks in discipline, it has no real planning behind it, and it gives cowards a chance to run away from the battle. My strategy won't let timid sailors man the cannons of Dutch ships."

The first officer looked surprised. "I didn't know that you had an interest in war at sea, Sir. Where did you learn these tactics?"

De Ruyter smiled. "Well, I've always been a good student, you know. Actually, I have noticed that land battles are becoming more complex, and with concentrated cannon fire and precise formation fighting, battles at sea could be conducted in a more organized way as well. I'm just working on it all. Just working."

De Ruyter rolled up his papers as his officer left, shaking his head. He had not told his first officer that he had been working on sea charts as well. Careful studying of the maps that were available had taught him that they were full of errors. For instance, the Caribbean Islands lay more than a hundred and thirty miles farther to the east than the Dutch maps and charts indicated. Some land masses were much larger than the maps showed whereas others were smaller. The whole seagoing business was inaccurate and lacked discipline. Fighting at sea was like an eight year old boy running around looking for trouble without realizing the risks. He wanted to change all that.

The next day brought some excitement and danger that De Ruyter had somehow hoped to avoid. Early in the morning the man in the crow's-nest had yelled, "Ships due west!" and Captain De Ruyter had run to the railing. They were ships, alright, but not ordinary ones. There were three of them, Dunkirkers. Pirates. They sailed in fast ships that were heading for the Dutch merchantman. This time he had a better crew. De Ruyter knew that he could depend on these men to do their duty. His orders were brief and clear.

He would use one of the new strategies he had designed and see how it worked during real combat at sea.

As the ships came closer, De Ruyter noticed that two of them were pirates, but that the third one was a captured merchant vessel whose nationality was unclear — the pirates had taken the ship's standard. He shouted orders to his grinning helmsman, an impressionable youngster who revered his new captain.

De Ruyter's ship wheeled and headed straight for the nearest pirate as if it wanted to ram it amidships.

The move caught the pirate captain off guard. Michael De Ruyter's reputation as a pirate hunter had preceded him. The pirate realized that it was De Ruyter himself that he had tried to attack. He backed off and ran for the safety of the coast. The other pirate followed, leaving the captured merchant vessel floating around without a crew. De Ruyter wasted no time. He ordered his men to quickly fasten a line to the ship and after this was done, he sailed back to the port of Flushing with his prize in tow. Since he had recaptured it from pirates, the ship was legally his. Its cargo would fetch a huge price on the docks of the Flushing seaport.

A few days later he set out again. After an uneventful trip across the Atlantic, he reached Brazil where he purchased goods for Seigneur Lampsens. Then he sailed on to some small islands of the West Indies, buying goods at every stop he made. With his ship lying low in the water De Ruyter returned to port. Seigneur Lampsens was pleased with the wares De Ruyter had purchased and realized that the young captain was not only an excellent sailor, but also an honest and clever businessman.

De Ruyter went home as quickly as he could and enjoyed a few days of rest with Cornelia. He delighted in sitting in his huge chair near the window and thought it a great honour that passersby greeted him. Often he waved at them, but more often he stepped outside for a friendly chat. Sometimes the people he spoke to were important citizens of the town. Still, he particularly prized his conversations with common people because he knew how much down-to-earth wisdom many ordinary people possess.

On Sundays he took his wife by the arm and together they walked to church. He was a very handsome man and wore his best clothes. Yet he didn't do it out of conceit. He realized that going to the house of the Lord required people to dress in their best clothes. He also gave generously to the church and knew that the money he gave was his own gift to the Lord Who had so wonderfully protected him during the weeks gone by.

During the year 1644, when De Ruyter was thirty-seven years old, he had saved enough money to purchase his own ship. In January, he approached Lampsens about one of the seigneur's smaller cargo vessels. At four hundred tonnes, it was small, but it was fast and very manoeuvrable. It was a triple-masted ship — one main mast amidships with a smaller navigation mast on the aft deck and another sail near the forecastle. This vessel sported ten medium-sized cannon and a hold that was suitable for carrying cloth and spices.

To De Ruyter, it was a dream come true. He knew that his parents would have been proud of their son, the captain of his own ship, the *Salamander*. He chose to rechristen it after the legendary lizards that were said to be able to walk through fire without being harmed. If this ship could survive enemy cannon fire unscathed, it would earn its name.

Although he still carried cargo for Seigneur Lampsens, he also started doing business for himself. He began sailing all over the world to purchase goods that would fetch a good price on the docks of trading cities. Since his wares were of a fine quality and his prices fair, he soon became known as a merchant who could be trusted.

One day, as he was on a return voyage from South America, he continued sailing along the coast of Africa in a northerly direction. He did this for a good reason. Captains returning from the Americas would cross the Atlantic Ocean where it was narrowest to escape many of the fierce storms for which this Ocean was feared. They would then continue the homeward journey by following the African coastline.

On this particular trip, he sailed along the coast of Morocco with the purpose of doing some business in the Moroccan port of Salee. Suddenly a huge suspicious-looking vessel changed course and began to approach the *Salamander*. He discovered too late that the suspicious ship was that of a notorious Spanish pirate who carried so many cannons that De Ruyter would stand no chance should he be drawn into battle. There was little time.

The pirate had cut off the speedy *Salamander*'s only escape route. De Ruyter changed his plan. He remembered the old saying that attack was the best defence. He turned his ship around and sailed straight for the attacking vessel. For just a second, as he stood on the deck of the *Salamander* and watched the Spaniard loom closer and closer like a cliff, he thought of the Rat.

Because of the freight it carried, the *Salamander* lay low in the water. This meant also that the cannon would fire close to the water and De Ruyter decided to use this handicap as an opportunity. As soon as his ship came close enough, he ordered his men to fire. The cannonballs hit the Spaniard just above the waterline with such a force that the big ship began to sink almost immediately. A huge cheer went up from the deck. The men began to sing out and danced for joy. They were sure that their captain would just sail away, but he had different ideas. The pirate crew had jumped overboard and would certainly drown.

De Ruyter ordered his sloops to be lowered into the water and to pick up every survivor. Even the captain of the huge pirate vessel was saved and quickly brought to him.

"If the roles had been reversed," De Ruyter asked the captain, "would you have been just as kind to me and my people as I have been to you?"

The Spaniard was a proud and cruel man. "I would have let you and your dogs drown," he replied.

This upset De Ruyter and he felt his temper reach the boiling point.

"Throw these men overboard, all of them!" he shouted while he turned his back upon the surprised Spaniards.

Immediately some strong sailors grabbed the pirate and some of his crew, but now the captain and his men fell to their knees and begged De Ruyter to show mercy. De Ruyter just nodded and then raised his hand to stop his men.

"I will save you and your men from death by drowning even though you are a pirate of the cruellest sort. I will give you your lives because I am a Christian. My God does not allow me to take a life, not even yours."

With so many Spanish prisoners on board De Ruyter could not allow himself to enter the harbour of Salee and he crossed to the southern coast of Spain instead. Two weeks later he safely entered the harbour of Flushing again.

# CHAPTER TEN

## *PIRATES AND BUTTER*

The next trip brought De Ruyter to the coast of North Africa again. As he approached the bay that led to the port of Salee, the captain of a passing ship informed him by means of flag signals that the admiral and the vice admiral of a fleet of five pirate ships were waiting for De Ruyter in order to take revenge and to rid the waters of the one and only pirate-fighter they feared.

Just an hour later Captain De Ruyter realized that the five pirates had hemmed him in and had made an escape impossible. But since it was evening, De Ruyter knew that an attack would not take place until the next morning.

Immediately De Ruyter divided his crew into two groups. The first was to go to their quarters to get as much rest as possible. The other group was to make the ship ready for battle. This involved loading the cannons, stacking cannonballs, securing loose objects, the checking of the rigging, and the preparation of enough food for the next day. De Ruyter worked alongside his men and wore his favourite sailor's clothes. He helped wherever he could and cheerfully encouraged his men to do their best.

When the first morning light coloured the horizon, he went to his cabin for his morning devotions and prayed fervently for himself and for his crew. Then, he stepped outside and gave his orders for the day. All men ran to their battle stations, the sails were hoisted, and soon every one was ready to face battle.

Once more De Ruyter went on the attack. It had worked well for him when he was still the obnoxious lad that roamed the streets of Flushing and it had given him the advantage in previous encounters with the pirates.

The *Salamander* sailed directly for the admiral's ship. The pirates on board had not prepared for an attack and only the lookouts were on deck. Even before they could ring the alarm, the cannons of De Ruyter's vessel spewed their deadly power. Cannonballs rocketed through the timber and the riggings of the enemy. The first volley had already been deadly, but it was not enough. As soon as the *Salamander* had passed the clumsy caravel, it turned around and passed the pirate on starboard, again inflicting terrible damage. Mast tops crashed to the deck, the ship began to list badly and began to take in water. Its decks had been pulverized and its cannons bent and scattered.

Now the crews of the remaining four ships scurried to get ready for action. The pirates' ships were strung out over a considerable distance with only the ship of the vice admiral floating close by the *Salamander*. De Ruyter didn't give it a chance to prepare adequately. Again he sailed right toward it, passed it on starboard and repeated the infliction he had given to the admiral's ship.

The pirates now noticed how easily the *Salamander* could be manoeuvred. They also saw their own two ships severely damaged whereas absolutely no damage was done to the Dutch ship. They retreated as quickly as they could.

On board the *Salamander* the men once again cheered and danced for joy. Who had ever heard of one little ship thrashing five large warships?

De Ruyter stood on the quarter deck and smiled. He was happy and thankful. Though he said little, he realized that the Lord had given him talents to work with and he knew that the victory didn't really belong to him. He was merely what the people called "a skipper next to God." The victory was God's, not his.

Then he gave his next order, "We'll sail into port to do the business we intended to do."

As the ship sailed deep into the bay and began entering the harbour, De Ruyter's men saw a frown etched on his face. A large crowd had gathered near the water's edge to watch the battle. At first, they seemed hostile. But they were instead excited about the fact that one little ship managed to defeat five larger ships that belonged to some of the townspeople.

The *Salamander* cast its anchor. A sloop was lowered and soon went to the dockside with a message to the Sant of Salee, the ruler of the town, the man who had allowed the pirates to use his harbour. He informed the Sant that he desired to see him in order to carry on the business for which he had come.

Soon the captain entered the sloop and as it approached the quay, the crowd began to cheer as if De Ruyter had been their hero instead of the man who had caused such enormous damage to the ships that had come from their own port and had sailed with the permission of the Sant himself.

The Sant received De Ruyter warmly and with great honour. When a few hours later the three remaining pirate ships cast their anchors in the bay, after having set their damaged ships on the beach, the Sant ordered the captains to be brought to him. As they stood before the Sant, while casting infuriated glances at De Ruyter, they received the sharpest tongue lashing they could have ever dreamed of.

An hour later De Ruyter was put on a horse for a triumphant ride through the city. The five defeated and exasperated captains followed him on foot with their heads bowed.

* * *

Like all good captains, De Ruyter took excellent care of his ship. Wooden vessels required extensive maintenance of the hull since the water could sometimes seep easily through the timber. To prevent this, ships were slathered with multiple layers of tar. The decks were scrubbed with sand and water on an almost daily basis. The riggings were cleaned and even the ropes were tarred. The sails were constantly maintained and often sailors climbed the rope ladders to inspect and mend wherever they found loose parts or even small rips in the canvass.

Most of the chores were done willingly, but scrubbing the deck was monotonous and detestable work. It was hard on the hands and wrists.

Captain De Ruyter still had his dog-eared Bible and he loved singing the Psalms. Often the crew could hear him singing when he helped with the daily chores. Soon they began joining him. At first it might have been just one or two men, but soon the singing of Psalms during deck scrubbing became a custom. Just imagine the feelings of an onlooker who observed thirty or so sailors doing their chores while singing the words of Psalm 135:

*Exalt the LORD, His praise proclaim;*
*All ye His servants, praise His Name!*

or Psalm 145:

*I will extol Thee, O my God,*
*and praise Thee, O my King;*
*Yea, every day and evermore*
*Thy praises I will sing.*

It is small wonder that the chore of scrubbing the decks was soon referred to as "Psalm-singing."[6] Neither did it surprise people to hear that the *Salamander* was the cleanest ship in any port.

Although Captain De Ruyter always wanted his ship to be 'ship shape' and clean as a whistle, there was one occasion on which he ordered it to be turned into a total mess.

---

[6] The term "Psalm-singing" for the scrubbing of the decks was still commonly used a few decades ago on the ships of the Royal Dutch Navy.

It happened during the return leg of a trip to Ireland. The *Salamander* entered the English Channel with a very valuable cargo in its hold. The weather was rainy and foggy, and it was early in the evening. The weather and nightfall prompted him to enter the harbour of Portsmouth and stay there until the next morning. He was surprised to find many Dutch vessels at anchor and learned that they were returning from a voyage to the Spice Islands.

The presence of so many ships with rich cargoes on board had also reached the ears of the Dunkirk pirates. Soon after the *Salamander* had cast its anchor, the waters of the Channel teamed with Dunkirkers who were patiently waiting for any Dutch merchantman to leave port.

The Dutch captains decided to wait for a few days. Eventually, they reasoned, the pirates would have to back off. De Ruyter, though, was eager to go home and waiting was very costly. Every day on the water he had to pay his crew, even if they were waiting in port. Back in Flushing the merchants were wondering where he and his cargo were. More importantly, Cornelia was waiting and De Ruyter was anxious to see her and to be with her and their first child.

After having waited for two days De Ruyter felt his patience grow thin. He just had to find a way out of this mess.

As he walked one morning, grousing about the pirates with other captains, he noticed a ship unloading its cargo. Sailors busied themselves rolling barrels from a ship to a barge lying some distance from it.

"What have you got there, mates?" he asked, nonchalantly.

"Rotten butter, Sir. We have waited too long and the stuff got spoiled. It's stinking now."

Then a sudden grin came on De Ruyter's face. He just had a most marvellous idea. It was something that could work, especially now the sky was darkening and a strong wind came up. He walked over to the skipper of the barge and told him that he wanted to buy three barrels of spoiled butter.

"Beg your pardon, Sir. Did I hear you say that you wanted to buy rotten butter?"

"You did, my friend. Just tell me the price and I'll pay you on the spot. Then you can have a few of your boys deliver the purchase to my ship."

The skipper scratched behind his ears and looked puzzled. "How can I charge you for something that has no value, Sir? Not even the barrels themselves are good anymore. You can have them, if you wish."

De Ruyter thumped the confused skipper soundly on the back and showed three strong fellows where to deliver the bizarre gift.

For their part, the *Salamander's* crew did a fair bit of head scratching when they saw what their captain had done. Some shrugged their shoulders, but others suspected that De Ruyter had something up his sleeves and decided just to play along.

"No, no! Those kegs are not to be put into the hold," De Ruyter hollered, "leave them on deck. We'll need them."

Then he stepped on board and ordered the sails to be hoisted. The crew didn't understand it at all. "Captain, the place is just swarming with pirates," one man said. "It's suicide."

"Suicide, my boy? Not at all! We're going home," De Ruyter answered cheerfully. Then he explained his plan in every detail. The men first listened silently, then they began to laugh. What an idea!

As soon as the ship had cleared the harbour lights, the barrels were broken open. Sailor after sailor stuck his hands into the yellow, stinking mess and took out huge scoops. Within minutes the railing, the deck, and the upper part of the hull were gilded with the gooey, yellowish mess.

"On your socks, men. Take your shoes off!" De Ruyter ordered.

Then the little cannons that could fire across the decks were loaded with grapeshot: little bits of nails and bolts designed to scatter over a wide area. The crew, clutching blades and muskets, crouched low to hide from view.

"Ship ahoy!" the man in the crowsnest yelled. De Ruyter took his spyglass and scanned the horizon as best he could. It was getting dark now and there was a strong wind, but there was also a Dunkirker in sight.

As the two ships got closer to each other, De Ruyter could see pirates gathering on the deck, ready for action, but when the vessels came close enough to one another to use their cannons, the pirates were surprised to notice that the strange merchantman was not firing and that no sailors could be seen.

"Where's everybody?" one pirate asked his buddy. "Things look spooky."

"Nothing spooky, my lad, they're coming back from the East an' have lost most of their men. Hardly no crew, my lad, hardly no crew, that's what it is. It's an easy take, this one. Yes, that's what it is. An easy take. Just wait an' see."

The other fellow didn't answer much. He didn't quite trust the situation. Since it was a Dutch ship, you could never be too sure.

"I don't trust them cheeseheads. They've always got something up their dirty little sleeves."

Of course he didn't know it, but he was right and would soon find out just how dirty the Dutchmen's sleeves had become.

The pirate captain ordered his cannons to be fired and he, too, became puzzled when the *Salamander* didn't respond. He thought that his opponent was short of manpower and proceeded by commanding to board it. Large hooks, fastened to ropes were thrown onto the deck of the Dutch vessel and as soon as the hooks found a strong grip, pirates began to pull hard so that the ships were forced close to each other. With a dull thud the vessels made contact. At that moment, dozens of hands reached for the *Salamander's* railings. Many pairs of feet pushed bodies in the air to scale the woodwork. Several did not even make it to the deck.

De Ruyter's ruse was proving clever. Comic, even. The pirates' hands slipped on the slimy butter and, with terrible screams and curses, they splashed into the water between the ships or skidded clumsily on the deck where De Ruyter's men picked them up and threw them overboard. The ones that managed to stay on two feet soon slipped and fell as the

*Salamander* pitched in the waves. Others stood with their arms spread like children do when they are on skates for the first time. They, too, were quickly shoved overboard by the grinning Dutchmen and within just a few minutes the pirates realized that they had become victims of a clever enemy.

"Told you, didn't I?" one of them wailed as he hurriedly sought safety against the bullets fired by De Ruyter's men from their hiding places. The pirates panicked and their own men cut the ropes to untie the ships from each other. Then the pirate captain gave the order to flee.

From his favourite spot on the poop deck, De Ruyter watched the pirate vessel move away. There was an enormous smile on his face. His trickery had worked miraculously well. But he was thankful, too, for he knew too well that there was Someone who had been at his side all the time to protect him and his crew.

In the meantime the winds were increasing in strength. De Ruyter ordered some of the sails to be lowered to prevent them from getting torn and ordered his helmsman to head for home. They didn't have to be afraid of pirates anymore since these evil sailors could not operate safely in this kind of weather.

A day later, De Ruyter's merchantman entered Flushing again. Hundreds of people waited for them and cheered instantly as they saw the ship negotiate its way toward them. Some folks made jokes about the dirty-looking vessel and others pinched their noses because of the smell, but all were happy and proud. The captain of that vessel was a creative one who possessed more than just one bag full of tricks.

Cornelia stood in the welcoming crowd. Above all things she was happy to have her husband home.

# CHAPTER ELEVEN

## *NOT ALWAYS BY THE CANNON'S MOUTH*

Over the coarse of years that De Ruyter had been the owner of the *Salamander*, he had become a well-to-do man. Seigneur Lampsens, now an old gentleman, considered De Ruyter a friend whose advice was always welcome. It felt good to have him around.

The Seigneur's son, who was to inherit his father's estate, urged De Ruyter to consider buying a larger ship. After all, compared to other merchant vessels, the *Salamander* was small, had a crew of a mere twenty, and could become the victim of pirates much easier than larger vessels.

But De Ruyter had shaken his head. "No, Seigneur," he had replied, "my ship does just fine. It is very fast and it is not always important how many goods you carry. I'd rather buy smaller and more valuable goods that will give you handsome profits."

The younger Lampsens didn't argue the point. He thanked De Ruyter for his fine services and left it at that.

The people of Flushing admired *their* captain. They realized that it was good for the town to have a man whose fame was spreading far and wide. And still, despite his fame and his wealth, he remained in touch with common folks.

One Sunday De Ruyter walked home from church with his youngest child, Engel, on his arm and accompanied by Cornelia and the other three little ones: Adrian, Neeltje, and Aaltje. Old Simon Nelisz walked with him. Simon had been a sailor during his younger years and now lived in a little house near the harbour, after he had lost not only his wife, but also his two children.

"The Lord has blessed you, Captain," Simon began, "and yet you are still one of us. That is what we like about you. You're still one of us. You're . . . humble. Yes, that's the word. You're great and yet you're humble."

De Ruyter smiled. "I have to be humble, Simon. There's nothing we receive by our own strength, you know that. Everything we have is God's gift to unworthy fellows such as I."

Simon nodded his head in agreement. "I know, I know. The Lord made you great because you're humble and not the other way around. But I wonder; the pirates fear you. You must like that."

At first De Ruyter didn't reply. "I am a business man, Simon, not a fighter. I don't like battles whatsoever. But I must protect my men and my business. You cannot have the one and not the other, I suppose." As he said this, he realized how many of his countrymen would do anything to obtain riches. They would even shed blood and commit murder for it.

De Ruyter preferred to stay away from armed conflict. He believed that when a man has found peace with God, he should also be a peaceful man in his dealings with his neighbour. And everyone he met was his neighbour. But he also realized that the other person would not always treat him in a way that the Lord would approve of. Still, he firmly believed in the faithfulness of his God and, to the best of his ability, would never allow himself to treat his fellow man in a manner the Lord would not approve of. He enjoyed going to church, speaking with ministers about matters pertaining to the service of God, and teaching his children the fear of the Lord.

*　　*　　*

The sun was shining on the blue Mediterranean. De Ruyter's sailing through the English Channel had been uneventful, especially now that the Dunkirk pirates had obviously decided to leave the Flushinger alone. Even the Bay of Biscay had given no difficulty. The *Salamander* had passed through the Strait of Gibraltar and was now on the open waters of the Mediterranean Sea.

The Seigneurs had loaded the *Salamander* with wares that merchants along the northern coast of Africa prized and they had ordered De Ruyter to trade these for delicate linens and spices.

The Mediterranean was yet another hotbed of piracy. Knowing this, De Ruyter kept his crew on high alert. One had to be careful.

A few hours later, with the rock of Gibraltar still in sight behind them, the crew heard the man in the crow's-nest yell that some ships were approaching at high speed. A little later the captain took his spyglass to observe the strange vessels carefully.

"French. They are French and this means that they might be pirates," he grumbled.

French ships were known for their great speed. It would be useless to try an escape. There were five of them and each was well equipped with cannons. It seemed as though De Ruyter would never face anyone on even terms.

De Ruyter's men had their weapons ready and the cannons loaded. They waited for their captain to give the command to start firing. But he didn't give the command. He knew that the time it would take to reload the cannons was too long to be effective against so many pirates. Unlike the engagement at the port of Salee, there was plenty of room for the other ships to manoeuvre. He noticed that the pirate ships had encircled the *Salamander* and he decided to try a different tactic.

"Lower the sails!"

This meant stopping the ship! The men looked at each other in amazement. There was a stunned silence. Was their captain ready to surrender? That would be foolishness, for the pirates would either kill them all or capture them and sell them as slaves to the Muslims that lived along the coast.

"Lower the sloop!"

This was too much. The captain was crazy. "Captain," the boatswain told him, agitatedly, "that's suicide!"

De Ruyter stepped into the sloop and just looked his boatswain in the eyes. "Maybe it's suicide, or, maybe it's not. I'm going to talk to the French commander."

Boatswain Houtens just shook his head. He hoped that the captain knew what he was doing.

The Frenchmen were just as surprised and confused. Through their spyglasses they saw that the captain of the little Dutch ship was actually being rowed out to them and could not figure out what this meant.

"Let him come. Don't shoot," ordered the commander. Then he went to his cabin to await De Ruyter's arrival.

A few minutes later his guest climbed the ropeladder, stepped on board and walked straight to the captain's cabin. He politely knocked on the door and walked in.

He stood in the hot quarters with his felt hat in his hand and with his legs spread shoulder-width apart. There was no fear in his posture as he, with a fiery glitter in his eyes, looked at the man seated behind the table.

"Michael De Ruyter, captain of a friendly vessel. You must know that your country and mine are at peace. I demand an apology and the guarantee of a safe passage."

The other looked up. "De Ruyter himself? Quite an honour, I must say. I am Commander De la Lande and I don't care for the so-called peace between France and your folks." Then he burst into a chilling laugh.

De Ruyter tried to keep his composure. In polite but firm tones, he informed the pirate of his intentions and of the sad consequences that might follow for the commander should he remain hostile to him.

Again the pirate laughed. "Nobody can touch me here," he replied. "Not even Michael De Ruyter!"

A sudden thought flashed through De Ruyter's mind. "You're laughing and you're making fun of me, but I'm disappointed in your behaviour, Commander. It's always been customary to offer a visiting captain a drink."

For a second the commander looked surprised. The Dutchman was changing the subject, but he could not figure out why.

"I have lots of fresh water on board and I carry the best French wine, of course. What shall it be, water or wine?"

It was the response De Ruyter had hoped for. "Sir, if I am a prisoner, give me water. But if I am a free man, give me of your good wine."

The Frenchman looked at De Ruyter and arched his eyebrow. He seemed angry at first, but slowly a smile worked its way across his face. Then he stood up, walked over to De Ruyter, and put his hand on De Ruyter's shoulder. "You're a real man, Captain. You have courage and a quick mind. That's why I'll give you wine to drink." Then he called for his cabin boy and ordered wine to be brought.

Soon the two were exchanging news and discussing world politics like a couple of old friends. After about an hour De Ruyter stood up. "I have to bid you farewell now, Commander," he said. "I have business to attend to and my crew will be wondering what takes me so long."

Minutes later De Ruyter left the big vessel the way he had come. Back on board the *Salamander* the men could not believe what had happened.

"The Lord was for us, and when He is, who can be against us?"

"That's what Paul wrote in Romans eight," one man remarked.

"Exactly, Teunis," De Ruyter replied. "Exactly, and don't you ever forget it."

With these words De Ruyter concluded the discussion on what had happened and soon the *Salamander* headed for the port of Salee once more.

As was customary, De Ruyter sent a few crew members ahead to the Sant of Salee with some presents and a letter requesting permission to sell wares on the city market. In the meantime, the captain let the crew know which items should be put on the deck to be taken to the market.

Things went well. The Sant not only gave his permission, he even indicated that he would come himself to see and judge the wares that De Ruyter was selling.

Later that day the two acquaintances greeted one another with all the gestures and words that were part of good manners in Salee.

Then the eyes of the Sant fell on a particularly fine piece of English cloth.

"I'll buy that piece for myself, Captain. Put it aside and take it to my palace later. I will pay you a fair price for it."

When De Ruyter paid his visit to the Sant, he was surprised to see that the man had invited his brothers and some high officials as well. After some more polite greetings, the Sant reached for the English cloth. His eyes shone as he stroked it with his hands.

"This is how much I will pay for it," he said as he looked at De Ruyter. Then he named a price that was much too low.

De Ruyter shook his head. "I am sorry," he replied, "but the value of this material is considerably greater than the sum you offered for it." Then he named the price.

The Sant stamped hard on the floor. "I've made you an honourable offer as my friends will agree and you don't have the right to ask such an outrageous price for it even though I could easily afford it."

"I know," De Ruyter answered quietly. "But I am under orders of the Seigneurs Lampsens to sell it for the price I mentioned. I may not and cannot change that."

"I'll keep you here until you soften up and accept my offer," the Sant continued angrily. De Ruyter could see by the bright purple colour on the man's face that he was totally serious.

"In that case you'll have to keep me here for a long time, Sir. My price is fair and I will have to stick to it."

Again the Sant continued to argue and just as firmly De Ruyter rebuffed him.

The Sant wanted to have it his way and began to threaten him. Now it was the Flushinger captain's turn to lose his temper and the result was that the two men continued to yell and scream at each other.

Then De Ruyter realized that he could not persuade the Sant to be reasonable and quietly said that he would give the cloth as a present, meaning that he would pay for it himself. But the Sant hit the table with his fist and shouted, "You may not sell it below the price for fear of spoiling the market, but you may give it away. I don't believe you and I don't want it as a gift for you're not my friend anymore."

"Certainly, I may not sell it below its value, but I may give it away if thereby I can avoid serious consequences," De Ruyter replied.

By now the Sant had lost his composure completely. "I'll have your ship confiscated, your crew sold into slavery, and I'll have you thrown into jail until you rot," he screamed.

"I know that you can do that, Sir," De Ruyter replied. "But soon the whole world will know that the Sant of Salee is a barbarian whose word cannot be trusted. It is easy enough for you to threaten me while I am in your palace, but on board my ship you wouldn't dare do it."

The Sant's eyes goggled. Without saying another word he stamped out of the room, followed by his guests.

De Ruyter was left alone. Certainly, he was upset and afraid of what might happen next, but he also knew that nothing could happen to him without the will of his heavenly Father. He took a chair right underneath a particularly opulent Persian tapestry, sat down, and waited.

One hour went by and nothing happened. Nobody came to see him and the Sant remained where he was.

One more hour went by. No messenger, no soldiers, no Sant.

Then, just at the moment that De Ruyter began to feel that everything was lost, the doors were thrown open wide and the Sant returned with his entourage.

"Are you ready to accept my offer?" the Sant wanted to know.

"My answer has not changed, Sir," De Ruyter replied as he stood up.

The Sant straightened himself, pointed at De Ruyter, and spoke to his followers, "Do you see this man, this Christian dog? Have you noticed how committed he is to his masters? Will you be as committed to me should the need arise?" Then he walked over to De Ruyter, took De Ruyter's right hand, placed it on his chest, and put his own hand on De Ruyter's.

"I consider it an honour to be your friend. I'll gladly pay your price. You have shown me what honesty and commitment are all about. You're not a dog but an honest man."[7]

Following his visit to Salee, De Ruyter went to other ports and continued to do business. Then the long trip home was begun once more.

On the return voyage there were no pirates and no storms. The crew was happy and thankful. De Ruyter knew that the Seigneurs would be pleased with the business he had done and he looked forward to being home for some time.

After the ship had been moored and the crew was ready to leave, De Ruyter noticed old Simon on the quay gesturing at him to come. De Ruyter was surprised but responded to the strange invitation.

"What's up, Simon?" he asked as he walked up to his old friend.

Simon said nothing. He had a sad and vacant look on his face. All he did was gesture to the captain to follow him.

They walked through familiar streets and although De Ruyter tried to have Simon tell him the reason for his strange behaviour, the old man didn't reply.

Suddenly De Ruyter noticed that Simon led him to the captain's own house. As they came closer, Simon walked even more slowly. De Ruyter's heart started to race. He knew that there was something very, very wrong.

Then he saw it. The De Ruyter home had been boarded up with rude planks. Straw had been strewn before the door as a sign of grief. A quarantine. Disease had spread through the house.

Simon stood still. "I am so sorry, so very sorry," he stammered. Then he bent his head and broke down.

---

[7] This incident caused the Moors to favour De Ruyter. They hardly wanted to do business with anybody else and would keep their goods for months if they knew that De Ruyter was coming again. In the time that De Ruyter made two trips other captains could only make one trip, often spending months trying to find wares to buy.

"Simon, what has happened?" De Ruyter asked in a quivering tone.

"When you were at sea your wife died."

De Ruyter swallowed hard while tears came to his eyes. "And the children?" he wanted to know.

"They're with some other folks for now. I am so sorry."

The captain stared at the crude planks over the door. Then he put his elbow against the door-frame and burst into tears.

It was another storm. But for this one De Ruyter was not prepared.

# CHAPTER TWELVE

## *BECAUSE THE COUNTRY CALLED HIM*

The days that followed were filled with sorrow and problems. To his friends in town, the ones that were used to calling at his door, it seemed that De Ruyter had suddenly lost his vigour. He walked more slowly, seemed to be lost in thoughts, and didn't even show an interest in his work.

Of course his friends understood. They realized that De Ruyter needed time to overcome his grief. They knew that he had to take care of his children first of all, since they were still too young to be left by themselves. De Ruyter had said that he didn't want his children to be divided among other families, that he wanted them to be together in a home so that he could be with them every time he returned from a voyage. He also realized that young children needed a mother to give them the care they needed so much.

De Ruyter went to discuss his problems with his pastor.

"My children need one another," he said. "They need to be together; they need a home. We're a family."

The pastor nodded. "You're a family man, De Ruyter. Your family has always been your first priority. Maybe you should look for a woman who has a lot of love to give, one who will make your children feel secure."

"But I have been married two times already, Pastor. One does not just hop from one marriage to another."

"I'm afraid that you have to choose between two possibilities. Either you have your children stay with strangers or you find them a new mother. Of course, you could always just give up the sea."

De Ruyter shook his head. "No, I can't give up the sea. You're right. There just isn't another solution."

And that is how De Ruyter began to look for a woman who would make a fine mother for his children. It wasn't an easy thing to do so he spent much time in prayer. The Lord knew about his plight and graciously provided when De Ruyter met Anna Van Gelder. She had become a widow when her husband, also a sea captain, passed away as a result of a severe illness when he was far from home.

A few months after his first visit, De Ruyter visited her once more and put the "big question" to her.

"Anna," he said, "I love you and I want you to become my wife and a mother to my children."

Anna looked at him tenderly. "I'd love to, Michael, I really would. But I don't want to be again the wife of a man who's always gone on voyages that are filled with danger. If I am to become your wife, you must meet one condition. Both your children and I want you to stay home."

De Ruyter reeled back in shock. "Stay home?" he asked. "I'm a businessman and I make my living on the ship I own. I love the sea. I have always loved the sea. You want me to give that up? I don't think I can." He hadn't expected this. He had expected Anna to go along with everything just as his first two wives had done.

"I know, Michael. But I know also that you have become quite well-to-do and that you can afford to stop working. You could sell your ship and continue your business from here, couldn't you?"

She had a point, De Ruyter knew. Hard as it would be to say farewell to his ship and to the oceans he had learned to love and respect, he could make a living as a landlubber. In the end, he decided that between a life on the sea and a life without this lovely woman, it was no contest.

"I will, Anna, I will," he answered.

A few months later, early in the spring of 1652 they were united in marriage.

They bought a home in Amsterdam and settled down in complete happiness. De Ruyter visited the harbour every day, and talked with old friends and acquaintances. He even sold the trusty little *Salamander*, his friend for so many years at sea. All the same, he began to enjoy the new chapter of his life as husband, father, and landlubber.

But something happened that would change his life dramatically.

The States General, as the government of the country was called, got into a dispute with the government of England. Oliver Cromwell, the leader of the English, felt that the Dutch were becoming wealthy at the cost of the English businessmen. He reasoned that the right to have the largest fleet of merchant vessels belonged to England and not to the people of the Low Countries. The States General felt that the English would soon begin a war with the Dutch, and they took the necessary steps to protect themselves.

It all became clear in the late spring of the year De Ruyter married Anna Van Gelder. A large fleet of Dutch ships was expected to return from the Mediterranean Sea with exquisite wares on board. Since the Dutch feared that the English might attack, they decided to send Admiral Marten Tromp with a number of warships to protect the Dutch vessels. But they instructed the hot-tempered Tromp to make sure that he would not start any hostilities.

The fleet of the English admiral Blake cruised up and down the Channel and met Tromp's ships. It was proof of good manners when ships properly greeted each other with signal flags and national flags. But Tromp was angry with the English already and ordered his men not to complete the greeting ceremonies. Now it was Blake's turn to lose his temper and he ordered his fleet to attack the Dutch.

At first Tromp tried to avoid the armed encounter, remembering that his government wanted to prevent a war with England at any cost. But when he realized that a battle could not be avoided, he responded to the attack with such ferocity that it looked as if Blake would be totally defeated. What saved the English was the approach of darkness. The two fleets became separated from each other, and both the English and the Dutch used the night to get a good rest and the next day to do repairs to their vessels.

The report of this incident soon reached the States General. The representatives met in an emergency session and quarrelled about whether or not Tromp had acted wisely.

The bickering about Tromp's actions didn't please the States of Zeeland one bit. They felt that strong action was needed to protect Dutch shipping and ordered a fleet to be made ready. What this really meant was that a number of merchant vessels were quickly equipped with more cannons. Crew members were guaranteed extra or "danger" pay. It was easy to equip the ships. What proved to be a bit more difficult was finding a commander. The name "Michael De Ruyter" was proposed immediately. The representatives agreed unanimously. De Ruyter was a great captain, a fearless leader, and he was a Zeelander by birth. What else could the States General ask for?

The States of Zeeland sent a delegation to Amsterdam with instructions to persuade De Ruyter to accept the command over the newly formed second fleet. The men chosen realized that theirs was not an easy task. De Ruyter was strong-willed and would not give in easily now he had decided to stay on land.

The men came to the De Ruyter home and found both De Ruyter and Anna willing to receive them. They tactfully let De Ruyter know that the States had appointed him vice-commander of the fleet. They told him that it was his duty to accept the position.

But De Ruyter didn't feel like it. "No, Gentlemen," he replied firmly, "I've done my duty, I have given my talents, and now it is my family's turn to receive all my attention and time."

Of course, Anna had helped to change his feelings. She was the one who had insisted that her husband stay home and now she was not going to allow him to break that promise.

"Gentlemen," De Ruyter said, "it is because of your foolishness that our army and our navy are in such a deplorable condition. You never wanted to spend money on the defence of our country. We have hardly any soldiers and our navy has not received any training, all because of your ignorance. Now you come begging me to do the impossible: destroy the English fleet. With what we have, we can't. What you're asking of me is that I sacrifice myself. If I do, it's on your conscience."

The delegates agreed. There was no point arguing about the state of the army and the navy. Things were just as he said. But there was no time to lose. They kept arguing.

"You're the only one who can help our country. Without you we will lose hundreds of ships and many hundreds of our men will be killed. Our economy will suffer immensely and countless people will be driven into poverty. You must help us."

De Ruyter looked at his wife. She just sat in her favourite chair and her eyes didn't give him any message. She didn't utter a word. Yet it was as if she were saying something. Her silence said, "It's up to you, Michael. You know how I feel. But our country is important, too."

De Ruyter stood up and fingered the scar on his cheek. He remembered how he had slipped and fallen on the deck in that first engagement long ago.

"I don't really want to do it, gentlemen. Yet because I realize that our country is in danger I will say yes. But I want you to know that this arrangement is strictly short term."

The delegates left his house very pleased. The fleet not only had a vice-commander, it had the best man for the job.

Little did De Ruyter realize that the most important part of his life's journey was only to begin.

A few days later De Ruyter went to the city of Flushing, this time to inspect the fleet and to put it into fighting order. He was happy to be "back home" again, but the condition of the fleet allowed him no time to visit old friends. He began training his crews immediately. The men didn't think this was necessary. They knew what was expected of them, they said, and they knew how to handle cannons, muskets, and all other kinds of weaponry.

De Ruyter, though, found it necessary to teach both the captains and the crews about strategy. "You just don't sail up to an enemy ship and start shooting," he told them. "The fleet has to work as a unit. Each captain should know exactly what to do and how to support his colleagues."

The time was short. Just a few days later the fleet set sail.

During his briefings with the captains De Ruyter had carefully explained the new plan of attack that he had developed over the years.

"No more attacking as a group and each captain picking an opponent," De Ruyter explained, using some ship models spread out upon the desk of his cabin. "When we attack, we line up behind each other and sail right through the enemy fleet. By so doing we'll cut them in half and cause a great deal of confusion. As soon as we're through, we'll split having the odd numbered ships make a circle to the left and the even numbered to the right and we'll attack them from the rear."

The captains weren't so sure that it would work. It had never been done before, but it was worth a try.

As soon as the enemy vessels came into sight, De Ruyter's plans were set in motion. Before giving his command to attack, De Ruyter went into his cabin to ask the Lord for His help. Then he went before the main mast to speak words of encouragement to his crew. Finally he went to his post on the upper deck. The battle was about to begin.

The ships lined up behind each other just as De Ruyter had said they should. From the distance the English didn't quite understand what was going on. Then the fleet attacked the English at top speed. As soon as De Ruyter's ship had penetrated the line of English fleet, it began to fire from both port and starboard. So did the ships that followed, causing incredible damage. The effect was a "cannonade." When a ship fired a broadside down the length of an exposed deck, the cannonballs skipped off the wood like a stone on flat water. The projectiles tore through everything in their path, often with bloody results. The English were totally confused and didn't know how to respond to the new manoeuvre, even though their ships far outnumbered the Dutch.

At this time another Dutch ship joined the fleet. Captain Douwe Aukes had reached the port of Flushing just after De

Ruyter's fleet had left. Having come back from the East, Aukes carried a hold full of spices. He had had his men unload these as fast as they could. Then he had some more cannons installed and away he went to help De Ruyter.

The problem was that Captain Aukes had not been briefed and didn't understand the new approach to sea warfare. But this Frisian was fierce and fearless. He drilled his ship at top speed right into a cluster of English vessels. Before he knew it, his ship received full punishment from the English cannons. He could see nothing but heavy smoke, leaping flames, and the breaking timbers of his ship. In desperation the crew called on him to lower the flag as an indication of surrender.

"Keep courage, children!" Aukes yelled. "When the situation becomes really hopeless, I will throw this burning stick into our gunpowder and I'll blow us all up to prevent the enemy from giving us a more terrible death!"

The crew knew well that Aukes meant what he said. With the greatest determination they threw themselves at saving the ship. An hour later Aukes was able to join his ship to De Ruyter's fleet.

The battle had started at about four o'clock in the afternoon. When darkness came, the English withdrew as quickly as they could to seek the safety of Plymouth harbour.

When this happened, De Ruyter called his crew members together. "When the Lord gives courage such as you displayed, He also provides victory. I thank Him and I thank you, my men!"

Later, Admiral Blake would write in his journal that De Ruyter was the only admiral in the world who rightly deserved the fame that came to him.

De Ruyter would not have agreed. "If the Lord is for us, who can be against us?" he would have said.

The richly-laden Dutch merchantmen could safely go home.

# CHAPTER THIRTEEN

## *A COUNTRY DISUNITED*

At home, Anna and the children lived in fear — fear for their father's safety. The De Ruyters knew that the English were very powerful, that they had a modern and well-equipped fleet and that the Dutch fleet consisted largely of converted merchant vessels. They feared that in spite of his courage and his intelligence Father De Ruyter was going to lose. Lose the war, lose his life. Everything.

Anna longed to have her husband home. She missed the sturdy man with his good-natured character and his deep voice. She missed his presence, his deep, throaty laughter, and his gentleness as much as the children did. The man who shouted out orders at sea, who bounded up to take his place at a cannon when a crewman fell was almost a different person in his own home. In many ways, De Ruyter had become much like his own father had been: strong, dependable, solid.

Sundays were empty without Father. When he was home he would dress in his best clothes and take his family to church. Then he would go for long walks with Anna and the children. Later, in the evenings, he would gather the children around him, take the youngest on his knees, and read to them. They loved the way he read. His deep voice made the stories of the Bible sound really exciting. He would ask them questions about what he had read and, before the children went to bed, he would pray with them. Then he would tuck them in, blow out the candle, and go downstairs. The children would listen to the squeaking of the stairs as Father went down and they would hear him talk to Mother. Soon they would fall asleep with a feeling of happiness and security. It was good to have caring parents and it was wonderful to have such a father as they had.

It looked as if he wasn't going to come home for a long time. The children prayed for safety and they asked that Father be allowed to come home soon, but deep in their hearts they knew that somehow their patience would be tested.

"Father will be back soon, right?" the children asked.

"I hope so. I don't know when he will come home. Only the Lord knows for certain just when," Mother answered.

* * *

In his cabin, De Ruyter had been asking the same question and his heart went out to his wife and children, but the business he had set out to do wasn't finished yet and he realized that it would take much longer than he had hoped. At first he had thought that it would be a matter of just a few weeks, but now he began to see that there were circumstances he had not counted on. And he began to worry about the things he could not change.

He worried about the English. They were a united and proud people. They had decided that England must be the most powerful naval nation in the world. They realized that they could not attain the position of being the most powerful without building a strong navy that would consist of fast and modern warships.

The Dutch were different, De Ruyter knew. They loved to do big business in the East and felt that their men were brave and clever enough to defend themselves. The Dutch had always been a somewhat peaceful people and thought that the English would leave them alone. They didn't understand the desire of the English to be the greatest naval nation on earth. As long as the Dutch could continue to do business, they were happy. However, when trade was interrupted, well, that made the Dutch furious.

De Ruyter knew all this. But there was something else he worried about. The Dutch were not united. Most of the common people in the country favoured the House of Orange that had ruled for many years. The great admiral Tromp had been an ardent admirer of the late Prince William II. But the Prince of Orange had died a few years ago and his son — William III, born a few days after his father died — was only two years old. Many people wanted him to be proclaimed Stadtholder[8] and appoint for the time being a representative of the Prince's family to rule the country. Instead there was a parliamentary system in place. The States General of the United Netherlands, as the parliament of the seven Dutch Provinces was called, had appointed Witte De With to be the chief commander of the fleet, instead of Marten Tromp.

Michael De Ruyter was a sea captain, not a politician. He felt that the good of the country should come first, and therefore he didn't openly discuss the politics of his time. He admired old Marten Tromp, and he had great respect for the talent of the chief commander Witte De With. But he did worry about the fleet. He knew that better, newer, and faster ships were needed. He realized that the crews should be properly trained, and he began to develop a plan to have the fleet strengthened by men who were not only good sailors, but who were also trained to fight on land.

These men would execute landings on the shores of enemy countries and strike swiftly against harbours and ships that were anchored there. Later in history these men would be known as marines, and they would have a long and proud history in the service of many different countries.

---

[8] A kind of Governor. The Princes of Orange were sovereign rulers of the Princedom of Orange, a territory in France. Later on this territory was taken by Louis XIV of France. More about William III of Orange can be read in the historical novels by Marjorie Bowen in the William & Mary Trilogy, published by Inheritance Publications.

For the time being, though, he had to work with what the States General made available. And he didn't like what he saw. The Dutch battle ships were converted merchant vessels, some of which were old and creaky. The fleet badly needed repairs.

*　　*　　*

At first De Ruyter had been the vice-commander of the fleet that the Zeelanders had put together. But since both the admirals Marten Tromp and Witte De With had been engaged in duties in other areas De Ruyter had fought his first battle in the service of the States General as commander.

While De Ruyter was in port, the fleet under Admiral Tromp was still far away. In order to reach home, Tromp had to fight his way through the English Channel, and the English fleet was waiting for him.

"The English have the advantage," Tromp said to his captains. "Their ships are much newer than ours and their crews are well trained. Now look at us. We've sailed around for a long time, our supplies are low, and we don't carry enough gunpowder and weaponry to defend ourselves properly. Our vessels are slowed down because they are dirty. What we have left is the Lord's grace and our own courage."

The captains nodded their assent. The fleet should have gone home much earlier, but the orders from the government had been otherwise. And the ships were dirty.

Because they were made of wood, parasites, barnacles, and other shell animals fastened themselves to the hulls below the waterline. In no time at all there would be so many of them that a ship would be much harder to navigate and would lose much of its speed. A dirty ship needed to be brought into port, rolled on its side, and thoroughly scraped. There was neither the time nor the opportunity. The Channel still separated them from the two fleets of Admiral De With and of De Ruyter. If Tromp would be united with them they possibly could keep the English at a distance and protect the merchantmen that tried to reach the safety of Dutch ports.

Tromp was a career sailor. As an admiral he was loved by his men. He never belittled anybody, he never used foul language, and he never cursed. He had a heart of gold and a character as strong as steel. It was to him that the sailors first gave the name *Bestevaer*.[9]

"Children," he encouraged his crew, "we must sail right through the enemy's fleet without engaging the English in combat. We have an appointment with De With on the other side! We must meet him."

And he did. Cleverly manoeuvring his ships close to the French coast, Tromp managed to pass the English unseen. A dense fog had helped him, people said later, but the cagey old admiral had answered, "Yes, but I needed that fog and I didn't send it. The One who did helped us through."

As soon as Tromp was united with De With's fleet, he was happy to see that De Ruyter was also there. Tromp had heard of De Ruyter, but he wasn't yet sure that this businessman-sea captain would prove himself useful in the fleet. In the end, he decided not to worry about it. As soon as he had lined up his ships, he received word that the States General had placed De With at the command of the fleet and that he, Tromp, had to serve under him.

De With was a good admiral, but he was disliked by his men. He was impulsive, had a bad temper, and treated his men with contempt.

De With decided that he would take command of the fleet on board Tromp's ship, the *Brederode*. But when he had himself rowed to Tromp's ship, the crew of the old admiral's vessel refused to take him on board. They even ignored Tromp's commands to do so. De With realized his predica-

---

[9] Best Father. It expressed how much the men loved their admiral. It was a name given to him because of his care and love for his sailors. Later the same name would also be given to De Ruyter.

ment and went back to his own vessel. Then he ordered the fleet to follow him in an attack on the English. Although both Tromp and De Ruyter had insisted that the fleet badly needed repairs and supplies, De With gave the order to attack.

Near the mouth of the Thames River the two fleets met. The battle was furious and brief. The Dutch were no match for the English and soon had to run for safety.

A month later the States placed the command once more into Tromp's hands, who promptly attacked the English and defeated them soundly. Now the merchant vessels could once more pass between France and England without being attacked by the English.

Tromp then sent a fast ship home with the request that he be permitted to bring his fleet home, and informing the States General of his desperate situation. The crews were tired and eager to go home.

The answer was disappointing. The fleet was not allowed to return home. Tromp received orders to seek out the English fleet and destroy it.

Tromp knew that he could not do it. Yet he had to obey the commands he received and approach the enemy's fleet. After the first cannons had been fired, a number of captains signalled that they had run out of ammunition.

Now Tromp decided to break away and seek the safety of home ports. The battle near Portland had become a disaster. With his ships severely damaged, his crew exhausted, and his captains angry, Tromp reached home.

* * *

"No country," De Ruyter wrote in his logbook, "has the moral right to engage its fleet in battle unless it has given its men the proper tools."

It was a lesson the Dutch found very difficult to learn.

# CHAPTER FOURTEEN

## *TRAGEDY AT TER HEIDE*

Nobody could say that the Dutch hadn't fought like lions near Portland. Nor could anyone say that the Dutch leadership had been inferior to the English admirals Ascue and Blake. The fault for the defeat lay with the States General. They had failed to provide the fleet with good ships and up-to-date weaponry.

The three commanders — Michael De Ruyter, Witte De With, and Johan Evertsen — marched grim-faced into the Flushing government buildings. In fact, they were so outraged that they had not taken time to clean up and, their faces still dirty from the smoke and the scorching flames of the Portland battle, they stormed into the building to give the ministers and dignitaries a piece of their minds. They were so upset that they refused to sit on the chairs that were hastily offered them. There they stood with their legs apart and their hands on their hips.

De Ruyter's deep voice thundered through the hall. He asked why the Council didn't show any interest in the honour and the safety of the country. He accused the councillors of looking after their own interests. They didn't care, he claimed, that hundreds of fine men had been killed mainly because the ships were old, dirty, and unfit for service. He asked the assembly why De With, Evertsen, and he should risk their lives any longer.

"I resign, gentlemen, I resign. Do it yourself and find out what it is like to get shot or blown up!"

Then he turned around and, followed by the other two commanders, strode out of the hall.

In the meantime, there was great joy in England. To taunt the Dutch, English vessels sailed close to the Dutch shores with brooms in the tops of their masts indicating that they had swept the oceans clean. Groups of children in the streets of London and Plymouth danced and made up songs of contempt for the Dutch.

Back in Flushing, De Ruyter's angry words had made a deep impression on the Council of Zeeland. First one and then another official rose to speak. They each acknowledged the truth of what De Ruyter had said.

Soon the Zeeland Admiralty agreed that something had to be done. It was decided to add new ships to the fleet, to increase the pay of the sailors, and to give bonuses to captains and crews who showed courage and bravery. Additionally, there would be ample supplies and all the ammunition and weaponry the fleet needed. A patriotic feeling began to sweep the country and this showed when rich merchants donated their own ships to the fleet and offered to pay for all the costs of warfare.

In the meantime, the English became even bolder. An English fleet under the command of Admiral Monk was seen passing the Dutch coast and it was obvious that the enemy was headed for the Dutch island of Texel where De With was gathering a fleet. But De With's fleet was not quite ready for combat. If Monk attacked, the outcome would be another disaster for the Dutch.

It was Marten Tromp, the old sea-dog, who had an idea. He would take his fleet out of the port of Flushing and try to engage Monk in combat. During that battle he would move his fleet into the direction of Flushing again, faking a retreat in the hope that Monk would fall for the trick and go after him. This would allow De With to take his ships out of port and attack Monk from the rear.

De Ruyter, in the meanwhile, had changed his mind. He was not going to let his country suffer shame and defeat while he was sitting in his cosy chair at home. As quickly as he could he went to Flushing to join Tromp's fleet before it set sail. Again he was placed in command of a part of the fleet, but this time he was in charge of the squadron that sailed ahead to be the first to contact the English.

* * *

Tromp's fleet numbered eighty vessels. Their crews were a determined lot who loved their old admiral and were willing to do all they could to maintain their freedom to trade across the seas.

The two fleets met near the coastal fishing village of Katwijk. A terrible battle ensued. De Ruyter's ship sailed at the head of the flotilla and was immediately attacked by a number of English vessels, some of which were much larger than his.

Thousands of people began to gather on the Katwijk beach to watch the battle. They stood there quietly, their hearts filled with fear and prayers. All through the country, the churches were filled with people for days of fasting and prayer.[10]

Four English vessels had managed to separate De Ruyter from the other Dutch vessels. They attacked with cannons blazing. Soon De Ruyter's ship was damaged so badly that it couldn't turn to fire its guns. Accurate English cannon fire had snapped off the masts. They had crashed over the decks. On port side the timber of the hull had been ripped open by gunshots and fire had broken out amidships. Yet at the very moment that all seemed to be lost some brave captains of

---

[10] On August 9, 1653, prayer services were held at 11:00 A.M. and 6:00 P.M. in the Kloosterkerk at The Hague. Also, after that, regular weekly days of prayer were requested (or commanded) by the States of Holland. In April 1665, the States of Holland again requested that weekly days of prayer be held. When it appeared that the eagerness for these days of prayer diminished, the States Council decided that the weekly half days of prayer should be changed to monthly whole days of fasting and prayer on the first Wednesday of each month.

other Dutch vessels came to the rescue and managed to drive the English attackers away. This gave them the opportunity to take De Ruyter's ship in tow and pull it to safety.

Suddenly, shouts of joy rang into the air. De With had managed to get his fleet out to sea and had come to the rescue. Monk gathered his fleet together and withdrew to make the necessary repairs to his battered ships.

The battle was not over. It would continue the following day. The night was used to make repairs and to prepare for the next morning — the Lord's day, Sunday, August 10, 1653.

By seven o'clock in the morning the two fleets met.

Tromp had lined up his fleet the way De Ruyter had done it previously and sailed like a wedge through the enemy's fleet. But instead of letting his ships describe half a circle, he merely had them turn around to once more cut through the English fleet. But this time Tromp paid the price. Somehow the enemy had anticipated the tactic. The English staged a singular attack on *De Brederode*, Tromp's vessel. Cannon and musket balls seemed to come from everywhere. Just as the old admiral was coming down a flight of stairs to assist some of his men, a musket ball hit him in his chest. As some of the crew rushed over to him, they heard him speak.

"I'm finished. Keep courage, men! Oh Lord, be merciful to me and to my poor people!"

All that the men could do was to carry the body of their beloved admiral to his cabin. The first officer signalled to the other ships that the captains should come on board. This was not an unusual request even during the thick of battle for there was always a lull in the fighting, which gave admirals a chance to consult with their officers.

De Ruyter was one of the first to come on board. By the silence of the men he knew that something terrible had happened. One of the crew accompanied him to the cabin and opened the door. De Ruyter took his hat off and entered.

Tromp was dead.

With his head bowed and his hands folded in front of his chest De Ruyter said, "Ah, I wished that I had died for him."

Centuries earlier King David had spoken the same words after he had been informed of Absalom's death. David had spoken the well-known words because he knew that his son had not been right with the Lord. Absalom had not given his heart to the Lord and when death came, it was too late to do so. Tromp, though, had been a God-fearing man. De Ruyter chose these words because he realized that Tromp had been a great leader, a man from whom De Ruyter had learned and could yet have learned a great deal.

The battle continued. The commanders decided to keep the death of Tromp a secret and to carry on as if the old admiral were still in command.

The battle raged on in all its fury. Again De Ruyter's ship was targeted, this time because the English noticed that there had not been enough time to make proper repairs to it. The English fired their cannons high, destroying the masts that had been repaired during the night. Once more other ships had to come to set De Ruyter free, and again he had his vessel towed out of the action. A few miles further they left the stricken vessel and returned to the thick of the battle.

Later that evening De Ruyter was informed that the battle had ended. He had realized this already since the cannons had stopped firing and their roaring had made room for silence.

Then one of the ships that had towed De Ruyter's vessel to the safety of darkness returned and the captain reported to De Ruyter.

"Were we victorious?" De Ruyter wanted to know.

"We lost many vessels, Sir, more than they did. If we were to determine victory by that standard, we lost. But the English did break the battle and left, so we assume that their damage must have been more severe than we anticipated."

"And *De Brederode*? What happened to it? If we didn't win the battle and if many ships went to the bottom of the ocean, what happened to it. It carried Tromp's body!"

"The English pressed hard on the admiral's ship, Sir. In fact, they were ready to board it, but we owe it to the Lord's grace and to the courage of Captain Pieter Florisz that it didn't happen. He sailed his vessel smack between the English and *De Brederode,* which saved it."

De Ruyter let out a sigh of relief. Tromp had often said, "If I die in battle, blow up the ship or throw my body over board, whatever. But don't let my remains fall into the hands of the English Redskirts."

The admiral's body was brought to shore to receive a funeral worthy of the man who had given his all for his country.

There was one more thing De Ruyter wanted to know. "Certainly, the English left, but why were we not clearly victorious? Is there something you haven't told me yet?"

"There is, Sir," the other replied. "Twenty-five of our captains deserted. They took their ships out of the battle and sailed home. They should be hung for this!"

De Ruyter's fists curled up, turning his knuckles white. The States would not prosecute the deserters. At best the captains would be given a reprimand. That's all. De Ruyter knew that they had fled because Tromp had been killed and De With (who was almost universally disliked) had taken over.

"The cowards!" De Ruyter shouted. "They dishonoured the memory of the greatest admiral we ever had!"

De Ruyter realized that the fleet was now clearly without a leader who had courage and intellect, one who was loved by his men. De With had courage and could measure up to most admirals, but he was not well liked by his men. Johan Evertsen didn't have the skills of Marten Tromp and he, Michael De Ruyter, was too young and inexperienced.

The country was in dire need of a man of character, skill, and courage.

# CHAPTER FIFTEEN

## *THE TURK WHO WASN'T*

The First Anglo-Dutch War (1652-1654) had come to an end and a peace treaty was signed. The English believed that they had won the war, but the stubborn Dutch replied that their ships could pass freely through the English Channel and didn't need to fear an attack by the Redskirts.

De Ruyter had once again said farewell to the fleet and enjoyed living in Amsterdam. Peace had returned and so had the prosperity that so many people had enjoyed before the war broke out. It allowed De Ruyter to continue doing business with faraway lands although he would now conduct his affairs from his office in Amsterdam.

Anna De Ruyter was possibly the happiest of all. She and the children enjoyed having their father home and it looked as if the future would offer them all the happiness one could expect.

One day a letter was delivered to the De Ruyter home which came from The Hague. After he had opened the letter, De Ruyter frowned.

"What's the matter, Michael?" Anna wanted to know.

"It's probably nothing, but the States General wants me to attend a meeting in The Hague."

"Did they tell you the reason?"

He shook his head. "They didn't. And if they have in mind to talk me into joining the fleet again, they're wrong. I've changed. I'm staying home."

Of course De Ruyter went to The Hague to attend the meeting, but when he came home a few days later, he wasn't smiling. The States General had bestowed a great honour on him. They had appointed him vice admiral of the entire fleet, but it had included the demand that he go back on board ship.

"You promised . . ." Anna began, but her husband waved her words away.

"I said 'no' once, twice, and three times, but the men kept on reminding me that a second war with England will likely break out sooner or later and used my patriotism to make me change my mind. I'm sorry, Anna, but my country needs me."

His wife turned her eyes downward. She wanted to smile, but she couldn't. She doubted that she would ever be allowed to live a happy life. Would she ever be allowed to have her husband come home from work every day and sit with her and the children at the supper table?

"I suppose this means that you'll leave tomorrow or the next day," she said, at length.

"No," De Ruyter answered. "I can stay home for quite some time. There's no immediate danger."

De Ruyter was allowed to stay home for some time. Yet, the weeks and months that followed brought fear and sorrow to the admiral's family.

Another plague broke out in Amsterdam. The illness struck without warning. It hit hard and without mercy. Within just a few days the first victims died. Soon it claimed tens of people each day.

De Ruyter's oldest son Adrian took ill with the fever. The next morning the young man died. He was barely eighteen years old. De Ruyter had named him after his own father.

Fearing that their other children might be attacked by the mysterious illness, the parents prayed fervently for the Lord's grace. They also prayed for themselves. The epidemic didn't respect a person's age or gender.

Following Adrian's funeral, De Ruyter changed. He spoke little and Anna found him time and again in deep thought. She knew that speaking to him would not help, so she merely placed her hand on his shoulder for support. He would manage a faint smile but not utter a word. Years later he confided to a friend that the death of his son had aged him by ten years. The tragedies that had beset his personal life had added up and taken their toll, even on a man whose faith rested securely in God.

A few days after the worst of the plague had passed, De Ruyter received orders to report to the admiralty. Spring had come, and the merchant fleet had left its various ports. It had sailed through the English Channel without incident, travelled across the turbulent Bay of Biscay, passed the Rock of Gibraltar, and set course for ports along the coast of Africa. It was there that pirates attacked them once more.

It wasn't long before the first reports of pirate activity on the Mediterranean Sea reached Amsterdam. De Ruyter understood why he had been summoned back to the fleet. Within a week he left port carrying orders to seek out and to destroy the pirates that had turned the Mediterranean into unsafe waters for Dutch merchant vessels. His orders also included that he put to death every pirate captain who had been guilty of killing Dutch sailors.

Yet the first ships he met didn't belong to pirates. The lookout in the crow's-nest yelled out that the approaching ships were warships, probably English. De Ruyter immediately took his spyglass and confirmed the report.

As the two fleets approached each other at full speed, De Ruyter ordered the cannons to be loaded with gunpowder only and to present a twenty-one gun salute. The English replied in the same fashion. Just a few months earlier the two fleets would have engaged in combat, but now they greeted each other politely. Then both fleets trimmed their sails and made time to have the captains visit each other. De Ruyter made a presentation of barrels of wine and beer and the English lavished the Dutch with spices. During the friendly conversation that followed De Ruyter learned where the pirates were hiding, and after both crews had waved to one another, the voyage was continued.

About two weeks later, after De Ruyter had replenished the supply of drinking water in one of the ports, the search for the pirates began in all earnest. De Ruyter split his fleet into four groups of two vessels each. The groups were to

spread out without losing contact with each other. This way a large part of the water surface could be covered.

Soon the outermost captains spotted a suspicious-looking ship that hastily changed course in an attempt to escape. The lead Dutch ships were built for speed and soon the suspicious-looking vessel was attacked and boarded. After a brief fight the pirates surrendered, were taken off their ship, and put into their captor's hold. Then the captain sailed for De Ruyter's ship and delivered the captives to him.

The pirate captain was a scruffy looking man whose shifty eyes betrayed a cold and cruel nature. He was led before De Ruyter who immediately began to interrogate him.

"Do you sail under the instructions of a country?"

"No."

"What is your home port?"

"Tetuan."

"Are you a Christian?"

"Not anymore."

"So you have forsaken the faith?"

"Yes."

"I hear that you have committed murder. Is that true?"

"Yes."

"One of your men said that you have sold over two thousand Christians into slavery and that some of these were your own relatives. Do you deny that?"

"No, but I don't think there were that many." The man didn't even try to hide his crimes and showed no remorse whatsoever. His eyes kept on shifting from one person to the next, from the tabletop to the beams of the ceiling.

De Ruyter rose. "I'm sure that you are the notorious pirate Arnando Dias. I'm right, I'm sure."

"You are." Dias turned his face defiantly toward De Ruyter.

"The admiralty of my country has instructed me to pronounce the penalty of death on any pirate captain who has committed murder and other bloodshed. Thus I order you to be hung. May the Lord have mercy on your soul. Do you have anything to say?"

Dias didn't respond. He spoke not a word to defend himself, neither did he utter a request for mercy. The man who had devalued the lives of many of his fellow men obviously didn't care for his own life either.

De Ruyter nodded at two sailors who promptly led Dias out of the cabin to the main mast where the execution took place minutes later. Dias' body was tossed overboard unceremoniously.

Within an hour's time the search for other pirates resumed.

Again De Ruyter didn't need to wait long. A Turkish ship, that seemed like a typical pirate ship, was sighted. Through his spyglass De Ruyter saw that it carried many cannons, that its riggings were of the kind that would increase its speed, and — what was more — that this so-called Turkish ship obviously had been built in Holland. Its design gave it away.

Once more the same two captains who had chased Dias began to pursue the pirate, who tried his utmost to outrun the two that were after him.

The pirate failed. Caught between the Dutch ships, the ship began to fire. The Dutch returned fire, unleashing enough cannon balls to cause serious damage to the pirate's hull. Then the pursuers zeroed in and boarded. A fierce battle took place on the pirate's deck, but when over a hundred of the pirates had either been killed or badly wounded, the captain surrendered.

A few strong sailors quickly put the pirate captain in chains and led him to Captain Van Zalingen. As soon as the pirate entered Van Zalingen's cabin, he began to chuckle.

"Are you from Amsterdam, too?" he asked.

Van Zalingen's mouth opened in total amazement. His captive spoke Dutch and came from Amsterdam! Van Zalingen wanted to say something, but he could not find the proper words quickly enough.

"Well?" the pirate wanted to know. "My parents live in Amsterdam, you know, near the tar gardens, across from the inn. Maybe you know them."

No shame. No fear. No respect.

Then Van Zalingen found his speech back. "So you aren't a Turk?"

"No."

"And you have lowered yourself to become a pirate?" Van Zalingen asked in amazement and disbelief.

"And why not? I've done it for years. It's an easy way to make lots of money and the risks aren't even that great. So why not?" The pirate was calm and so self assured that it was unnerving. He was a tall, gaunt man with thinning hair tied back in a ponytail. His shoulders, though, were broad and powerful. As he looked around the room, his eyes jutted wildly from his scarred yet somehow aristocratic face.

"And your name?" Van Zalingen wanted to know.

"Jan Leendertsen."

"Jan Leendertsen," Van Zalingen mused. The name rang a bell. A captain by that name had simply disappeared years ago. Everybody had thought that something terrible had happened to him. But nobody would have guessed that the man and his crew had joined the hated and feared Turkish pirates.

"To the admiral with this man. Quickly," Van Zalingen ordered.

A few men pushed the pirate out of the cabin, across the deck, and made him board a sloop. Then he was taken to De Ruyter. An officer had informed De Ruyter about the man who was to be brought before him.

When Leendertsen was pushed into De Ruyter's cabin, the welcome he received was hostile. De Ruyter stood menacingly in the middle of the room, unafraid of the pirate.

"I know who you are," De Ruyter barked. "My instructions read that I must hang every pirate captain I capture, and that includes you, of course." De Ruyter's face was as hard as stone.

"Are you a Christian?" he demanded to know.

Leendertsen shrugged his shoulders. "I was one at one time, I suppose. Like everyone else. But no, I am no longer one."

De Ruyter's eyes grew wide. "So you have forsaken Jesus Christ, the One who loved you enough to give His life for you?"

Again the pirate shrugged his shoulders. "Lots of people die, Admiral. I've killed a few myself. What does it matter?" Leendertsen was cleaning some of the dirt out from beneath his fingernails and flicking it, nonchalantly, on the deck.

"I suppose then that you have Christian slaves on board who do the rowing for you, chained to their filthy seats until they drop dead."

Leendertsen continued cleaning his nails, oblivious to De Ruyter's growing rage. "Fifty-two of them to be precise," he drawled.

De Ruyter stepped up to the tall man until he was close to Leendertsen's chest and shouted up at him, "Then we take you to your ship and we'll force you to undo the chains of each of them!" De Ruyter was shaking with rage. He had never met someone so completely unflappable.

Leendertsen was pushed out of the cabin. A few officers followed, wary of the big man, followed by De Ruyter. The men climbed from the one ship to the other and went into the hold where the slaves were kept, still chained to their seats. The smell was unbearable. There had been no place for the men to relieve themselves, and the smell of human waste and sweat mingled in the thick air. Only a bit of light entered through the holes of the huge oars the slaves had been forced to handle.

"Any Dutchmen here?" De Ruyter asked loudly.

The reply indicated that seventeen of them were indeed Dutch.

But then something strange happened. As soon as the chains fell off the poor men, they fell on their knees before De Ruyter, begging him to spare the pirate's life.

"He never had us whipped."

"He ordered his men to feed us decently."

"This place is filthy now, but he had it cleaned regularly."

"He's a pirate all right, but he's not of the cruel type."

"Please, Sir, spare his life!"

De Ruyter looked at the wretched men before him and scratched his chin pensively. He wanted to get these men up and into the light. He didn't want to spare this particular pirate, of all people.

"I will spare him," he said, "but only because of you. Yet I'll have him stand trial back home."

He ordered the freed men to be washed and fed, then turned his back to Leendertsen, and went back to his own ship.

"Never mind the instructions of the admiralty," he mumbled. "There are times that other instructions come first."

He smiled at the first man he met on deck, a young deckhand barely out of his fifteenth year. The boy was just beginning his naval career.

"How are you doing, Hendrik?"

"Fine, my lord Admiral, just fine."

"So am I," De Ruyter answered cheerfully. "So am I."

# CHAPTER SIXTEEN

## *TROUBLE NEAR THE BALTIC*

The admiral counted on being home for a few months. After all, the country enjoyed peace with England. The pirates who had caused much damage to Dutch shipping had stayed clear of the merchant vessels belonging to the Low Countries. They were afraid of angering the Dutch.

De Ruyter knew that the Dutch economy was fueled by the shipping industry. Hundreds of vessels carried cargo from one part of the world to the other. Dock workers, rope makers, sailors, and carpenters all owed their livelihood to the shipping trade. It wouldn't take much to jeopardize the industry again. England was always envious of Dutch prosperity. Besides the English, there were pirates who were always vigilant for fat Dutch ships. France and Spain, too, thought that the trading empire the Dutch had built up was just a little too successful for their liking.

De Ruyter thought that he could delight in his family and friends, enjoy his walks through the city and his talks with men that had sailed under his command. Like any sailor, he loved retelling the stories of his adventures, although he was always careful to mention where the real credit belonged.

His hopes of beginning a peaceful life were again dashed when news from Sweden and Norway sent a wave of fear through the seaports along the North Sea. Even Anna was alarmed and a little confused by the reports she heard during her trips to the market.

"What is the problem with the king of Sweden, Michael? Everybody is talking about the possibility of a war."

"King Charles X Gustavus of Sweden has big dreams. If he carries these out, much of our shipping into the Baltic Sea will be threatened," De Ruyter replied.

"I don't understand," Anna answered. "What great dreams could this king have?"

"I don't really know, to be honest. Some think that he wants to unite the descendants of the Vikings — he wants to include not only Sweden, but also Norway, Denmark, and the parts of Germany and Poland that touch on the waters of the Baltic into one big empire."

"Can he just do that? Wouldn't he find it impossible to build such a large empire without getting into war?"

"I'm sure that he's aware of the risks. But the man is very ambitious. In fact, he has said that he wants to include all of Europe in his plans. Mind you, I don't think that this would ever work, but the ambition is there."

"I shiver at the very thought of it," Anna continued. "I hate war and I don't see any use for it. In the long run, no one ever really wins."

"Like it or not, you can count on seeing some war preparations soon. Danzig, for example, is central to our trade. Our captains go there to buy grain. If King Charles Gustavus captures it, our trade with that city will come to an end, our ships will be taken, and many people here will lose their jobs. That's the bottom line."

Anna didn't reply. She knew that her husband often could foresee what would happen. His instincts were seldom wrong. King Charles Gustavus was more dangerous to Dutch shipping than a hundred pirate captains. She couldn't help feeling though, that lost jobs were better than lost lives.

Just a few days later a messenger delivered an envelope with new instructions for the admiral. A fleet was assembled to protect Dutch shipping. De Ruyter was to be the commander.

The fleet left port soon thereafter. Eight days later it reached the city of Copenhagen. There it met a smaller fleet of Dutch warships and together they sailed for Danzig.

In the meantime King Charles Gustavus had led an army into Poland and was ready to attack Danzig. The citizens of that city were overjoyed when they saw De Ruyter's fleet sail into port, but King Charles Gustavus didn't share the emotion. He knew all about De Ruyter — an opponent he would rather not deal with. He sent some swift messengers to De Ruyter to sue for peace.

The admiral didn't want war either. Under the terms of their treaty, the Swedes promised that the Dutch trade with Danzig would not be interfered with and that they would not attack it. The Dutch would be free to continue doing business with any city on the Baltic coasts.

The danger seemed to have been avoided and De Ruyter set sail again without having fired one shot. After a week of snow squalls, De Ruyter's fleet reached the safety of its own harbours once more.

But the other storms, the human storms of war, were not so easily overcome. Two years later, the admiral heard disturbing news upon his return from pirate hunting in the Mediterranean Sea.

This time it was King Frederick III of Denmark who started the war. The Swedes had captured some Danish cities earlier and now that King Charles Gustavus was engaged in a war with Poland, King Frederick thought that this was the time to recapture his cities.

He had barely declared war against Sweden when a period of very heavy frost arrived. It was so cold that even the salt water between Danish islands froze over. This allowed the Swedes to cross the frozen mass, even though Danish military strategists said that it was impossible. So it happened that the Danes became the surprised victims of one of the most daring military schemes of their age. After marching across the ice, the Swedes took some of the major Danish islands, thereby controlling the entrance to the Baltic Sea.

The conflict between Denmark and Sweden was, technically speaking, none of the business of the Dutch and it should have allowed De Ruyter to stay home. Yet for some reason, the Swedes broke their treaty with the Dutch. Messengers dropped off some letters at the De Ruyter residence. The instructions were clear: the admiral was to sail to Sweden once more, in order to gain a new guarantee that the shipping lines would remain open.

At first the Dutch sent Vice Admiral Van Wassenaar-Obdam to the troubled region, but when it became clear that the Dutch might be drawn into an armed conflict with the Swedes, De Ruyter was sent out too.

Near Kronenburg the first fleet was drawn into a battle with the Swedes. Although Van Wassenaar-Obdam succeeded in defeating them in a short battle, he lost two of his vice commanders and the unpopular vice admiral Witte De With.

That's why De Ruyter was sent out with a powerful fleet. His orders were to restore order and peace in the Baltic region.

The departure of De Ruyter's fleet caused quite a commotion in Europe. Both France and England considered that the Dutch were going too far. The "cheeseheads" should not think that they were Europe's masters. The English, who considered themselves masters of the sea, hated the thought of the Dutch ruling the waves. They, too, sent out a fleet. Its admiral was ordered to intervene and stop the Dutch from reaching the Baltic.

The king of Sweden liked that idea. If the Dutch and the English attacked each other, the Swedes could continue to conquer Denmark and Poland.

This worried De Ruyter. The approach of the English fleet meant that he was caught between the Swedes and the English, and this was a position he didn't want to be in.

Back home the Dutch and the English discussed the situation and after the English were satisfied that De Ruyter would not interfere with English shipping and that he would not attack the Swedish mainland, the English called their fleet home.

Since it didn't look as if military action would be required, the Dutch ordered part of their fleet under the command of Van Wassenaar-Obdam to return home. This vice admiral was happy to go home for it was bitterly cold and he suffered from crippling arthritis. There were days he could not even get up from his captain's chair.

De Ruyter wanted to go home as well, but he sensed that as long as Danish islands were held by the Swedes there could be no peace. Through communications with Swedish commanders he tried to persuade them to put an end to their war efforts and to go home, but the Swedes were not about to give up their quest.

Much to his displeasure De Ruyter now received orders to assist the Danes in driving the Swedes out of Denmark. De Ruyter was to take Polish and German volunteers on board and received orders to take these men to the city of Nyborg where they would land to recapture the city. The whole military operation would be under the command of the Danish admiral Bjelken.

The fleet cast anchor near the city of Nyborg where preparations for the landing began immediately. De Ruyter watched as he stood on the upper deck, but he didn't like what he saw. Soon he began pacing up and down while shaking his head in disbelief. The Danes were much too slow and it would take too long for the landing crafts to be loaded.

"We're giving the Swedes ample time to get ready," De Ruyter complained. "They'll be waiting for us on the beaches. We will never succeed."

He was right. When finally the first wave of sloops hit the sand of the beach, the soldiers found the Swedes ready.

Although there was no lack of courage, the Danes, assisted by Dutch, Polish, and German soldiers could not defeat the enemy. Soon the situation became hopeless and the Danish commander ordered his troops back into the sloops and back to their vessels.

De Ruyter was exasperated. He had foreseen that this would happen and he regretted the fact that Bjelken instead of he had been appointed as commander of the operation. Numerous men had been killed in vain. Much bloodshed could have been prevented had the element of speed been used.

The next morning Admiral Bjelken had himself rowed to De Ruyter's ship in order to give an explanation of what had happened. But as soon as he put his feet on the deck of De Ruyter's ship he was met by a livid Zeelander. De Ruyter scolded Bjelken with such an outburst of words that the Dane didn't get a chance to put in a word. When he finally succeeded in uttering some words of excuse, De Ruyter tore out his own hair with anger. "The blood of every dead man is on your head! You're incompetent and you should never have accepted the command!"

That same day the fleet raised anchor and sailed for Kortemunde. De Ruyter told Bjelken that he would assume command of the landing operations and the Dane was easily persuaded.

De Ruyter decided to have the sloops manned quickly, to row to the beach at top speed, and to have his troops dash for the city gates without any delay. Personally he directed the operation and while the last men were boarding the last sloop, he ran into his cabin, returned within minutes and, dressed like an ordinary sailor, jumped in. He ordered his sloop to go at the head of the expedition and he was one of the first to set his feet on the beach.

It didn't take long before the Swedes surrendered after having discovered that their enemy had come close to the city. A few weeks later the Swedes sued for peace and returned to their homeland. Never again did the Swedes and Danes battle against each other. It proved to be a peace that lasted.

The Danes were overjoyed and their king was so thankful for the outcome of the war that he presented De Ruyter with a gold chain and a medal, and elevated him into nobility. He also offered the Dutch admiral an annual income of 2000 guilders, quite a sum in those days.

After having cruised up and down the Baltic for the duration of the winter to make sure that no other hostilities would break out, De Ruyter sailed for home.

He longed to be home with his wife and family. He just didn't like war and he didn't enjoy being an admiral. All he wanted to be was a businessman living in Amsterdam.

# CHAPTER SEVENTEEN

## *FAR FROM HOME*

As the fleet rounded the southern tip of the island of Texel and entered the Southern Sea (which is now called the Yssel Lake), the weather had calmed down but the waters were covered by a dense fog. The admiral stood on deck keeping his attention focussed on the weather. Visibility had been reduced to just a few yards which meant that ships could easily collide with each other. The lookouts had received instructions to watch and listen. Although approaching ships could not be seen, they might be heard.

De Ruyter thought of home. He longed to be with his family and he hoped for a time of peace. In his heart he wasn't a man of war. He was getting older now and dreamed of working in his warehouses, meeting with businessmen, and spending time with his wife and children.

The fleet sailed on slowly and needed only a few hours to reach the port of Amsterdam. Just as the admiral was about to turn away from the railing to go to his cabin for lunch, a terrible accident happened. Seemingly from nowhere a huge vessel crashed into De Ruyter's midship, pushing it completely under water. The collision was so fierce that the admiral was thrown overboard. Because he was dazed and wore heavy clothing, he began to sink almost immediately. As he was being swallowed up by the water thoughts of his wife and family flashed briefly through his mind.

But then the Lord provided rescue. Two sailors who saw the admiral sink into the chilly water immediately dived after him, brought him to the surface, and had him lifted up by crewmembers of the vessel that had caused the accident.

Soon he stood on the deck. Water rained from his clothing. "I thank you, men. May God bless you richly," he said softly. Then he shook their hands, turned around, and went to a cabin to get a change of clothes.

That same evening he came home and with his wife thanked the Lord for safety. He knew very well that his life was always in God's hands. Many times he had read the words of Psalm 31:15, "My times are in Thy hand," realizing that the Lord controlled the day of his death and that no person or circumstance could change that.

He had hoped to stay home for a while, but again his being with his dear ones was something he could not control. And so it happened that one day soon after his return he was summoned back to board ship. The fleet had been kept in a state of readiness and the States General had once more been forced to call on the admiral to sail into the Mediterranean where again pirates had attacked and destroyed a number of Dutch merchant ships.

The fleet had barely sailed into the Mediterranean when something happened that completely changed the purpose of the voyage. The States general had sent out a fast-sailing ship to deliver an urgent message to the admiral. De Ruyter frowned when he read the letter. Then he just stared into the distance and thought.

The message was clear enough. The English had grown jealous of the great successes the Dutch had had in business. The merchants of the Low Countries had reached out into all parts of the world and their ships had returned to their ports laden with rich cargoes. This had resulted in a decline in the trade the English had engaged in and English merchants had begun to complain bitterly to their government.

Wars are terrible events in the history of man. Sometimes they broke out for religious reasons. At other times political events led to wars. Yet, sadly enough, sometimes even jealousy between one country and another would lead to bloodshed.

De Ruyter understood. Years earlier the English king Charles I had been beheaded. England had turned into a republic under Oliver Cromwell, and the young Charles II had fled to Holland. Throughout their history the Dutch had always given shelter to those who were persecuted and also Charles II was welcomed to the Low Countries. When some years later England ceased being a republic, Charles returned to his own country. The States General gave him valuable presents when he left, and it seemed that both England and Holland would enjoy many years of peace and co-operation. Yet it seemed that Charles had soon forgotten the kindness he had received, for De Ruyter learned from the message that war between the two countries could break out at any time. The English would not tolerate the commercial prosperity of the Dutch.

Problems arose almost immediately. A few days after De Ruyter had received the message, the lookouts reported that a large fleet had come into sight. A little later De Ruyter realized that the fleet was English under the command of Admiral Lawson. As was customary, De Ruyter ordered the English to be greeted with flag signals, but Lawson didn't return the gesture.

Now De Ruyter sent out a ship with instructions to visit the English admiral and to find out why he had not returned the salute. When the ship returned, De Ruyter found out that King Charles II had forbidden his admiral to show any form of kindness or politeness to the Dutch.

De Ruyter decided not to run away from the English. With his fleet he followed Lawson just to make sure that the Englishman would not attack Dutch shipping.

Then he received another message from the States General. It said that the English were assembling a huge fleet and that an army of fifteen thousand men stood ready to board the vessels. No, Charles had not declared war yet, but it seemed that a plan for an attack was clearly in the making.

De Ruyter went to his cabin and wrote a reply to the States General. "I understand your concerns," he wrote, "about the English and their preparations for war. But it is only man who threatens us. Who fears the power of the sword should not engage in battle. Therefore we shall silently wait and see what the Lord has in store for us." De Ruyter didn't fear. At one time, when in the heat of battle bullets and cannonballs were whistling around him and he saw how members of his crew were killed, he called out, "Why, O Lord, do they die? Why may not I die instead?" However, he had learned that the Lord's plan for one's life unfolds itself only one day at a time and that He does not give man much advance notice of what He will do with the time given to His creatures.

In the meantime it became clear that Admiral Lawson had no specific instructions other than to cruise up and down the Mediterranean. War didn't seem imminent. Yet when De Ruyter's fleet went into port to take in food and water, a courier arrived from Holland. The poor man had raced his horse for nine days in order to catch the admiral in time. He was totally exhausted when he handed the admiral his next instructions. At first De Ruyter didn't tell his officers what the fleet was to do next, but finally he made it known. "We're going around Africa to the Gold Coast, men."

Although there was no war, the English had captured a number of Dutch trading posts near the Equator, had taken the Dutch ships that lay anchored in the bay, and had successfully destroyed the Dutch trade with that part of the world. Now De Ruyter was summoned to recapture the posts, if possible without bloodshed, and to restore the trade that had been going on before.

After the fleet had arrived at the Gold Coast, the taking of the trading posts was indeed accomplished without firing one single musket. De Ruyter ordered the Englishmen on board an English warship that lay anchored there and sent them off to their country as free men.

By that time it was necessary again to look for fresh drinking water. The admiral sent one of his captains to shore with orders to speak to the chief of the native people and to politely ask him for his help.

Great was the surprise of the captain when the native chief spoke to him in Dutch.

"Who is the admiral of your fleet?" the chief asked.

"Michael De Ruyter," was the reply.

Then a big grin grew on the chief's face. "I was his friend!" he shouted in excitement. "I am Jan Company of Flushing. Bring me to my friend. Now!"

Moments later some sailors rowed Jan Company to the admiral's ship. De Ruyter watched them approach and wondered what it was all about. Through his spyglass he saw that his men were taking an old Negro to his ship, but he had no idea why. Maybe the old chief desired to meet him.

When Jan finally climbed on deck, De Ruyter didn't recognize him. After all, forty-two years had gone by and it was in the year 1620 that the two friends had seen each other for the last time.

Jan approached the admiral and blurted, "Michael, it's Jan. I am Jan Company!" De Ruyter was totally surprised. "Jan!" he called out as he hugged his old friend. Then the two disappeared into the admiral's cabin where they talked and laughed for many hours. They had done well, the two. De Ruyter was an admiral and Jan Company had become the king of a large tribe.

"You're still a Christian, I trust," De Ruyter said.

Jan nodded but didn't say a word. De Ruyter sensed immediately that something was amiss. "Remember, you were baptized in Flushing and the Lord God wants you to serve Him."

At first Jan didn't reply. "I still know the Apostles's Creed and the Lord's Prayer," he said finally, but his voice didn't sound very convincing.

"But that's not enough, Jan. You must love the Lord; that's what the Christian faith is all about."

"I know," Jan replied, "but my wife and my children laugh at me when I talk about Jesus and the men of my tribe don't take me seriously. Now I keep my faith to myself. I've tried, believe me, I've tried."

De Ruyter didn't find it necessary to add much. Jan knew where he had failed.

"And do you hope to return to Flushing one day?" De Ruyter wanted to know.

Jan shook his head. "No, I don't," he answered. "I'd rather stay in this poor country with its poor people. It is here that I hope to die."

Later that day De Ruyter ordered a large box to be filled with clothes as a gift to king Jan. Then the two friends parted for good. De Ruyter's eyes were misty when he saw the distance between him and his old friend become slowly greater. He felt pain in his heart because of his old friend.

The very next day food and water were brought on board. Then the fleet left for other destinations.

# CHAPTER EIGHTEEN

## *WAR WITH ENGLAND AGAIN*

De Ruyter sat at the table in his cabin. In front of him lay a large envelope that had just been delivered to him by the captain of a ship that had been sent out from Holland for the purpose of finding the Dutch fleet.

The envelope would contain new instructions, De Ruyter realized. He hoped fervently that the States would order him to return to home port for he feared that another war with England was almost unavoidable. The English had captured Dutch trading posts in Africa and even overpowered the Dutch colony in the New World. They had, while the two countries were supposed to have been at peace, taken New Amsterdam and had promptly changed its name into New York.

There was another reason why De Ruyter wanted to sail for home. The fleet he commanded was just a small one, good for chasing pirates and for small military operations. It was by no means capable of large scale sea battles. Supplies were running low as well and the crew was tired after the engagements around Africa.

De Ruyter opened the envelope and read the instructions carefully. A deep frown grew on his face when he realized that his concerns had been correct. The States ordered him to sail across the Atlantic to the New World to recapture the colonies the English had taken, yet the letter avoided mentioning the possibility of another war with England.

After he had read his instructions, De Ruyter thought of his country. Oh yes, the larger part of the Dutch fleet was still in port and its two commanders, Cornelis Tromp, a son of Marten, and Van Wassenaar-Obdam, were capable officers. But De Ruyter knew the English better and had greater knowledge of their strategies at sea than the other two, yet he was ordered to stay away making it impossible for him to give leadership in preparing the fleet for war.

Then he put the letter away, stood up, and summoned his captains for a briefing. The next day the crossing of the Atlantic began.

The fleet headed straight for Barbados, for that island also had been taken by the English. But when the ships came close to land, they were welcomed by fire from powerful cannons that the English had posted in anticipation of the arrival of the Dutch. The admiral therefore decided to turn his attention elsewhere. By now his supplies had become really low and his ships lacked the necessary gunpowder to be effective. Just the same, a number of English ships were captured along the way, but these didn't carry the supplies De Ruyter needed. There was no way he could recapture New Amsterdam and the best solution was to take the fleet home. Since he didn't trust the English, he followed the coast of North America to Newfoundland and began to cross the Atlantic toward Norway. From there he would sail along the coast in a southerly direction and try to reach Holland without being discovered by the English who must have found out that De Ruyter had just a few ships and lacked supplies.

Ever since he had left the coast of Africa, months had gone by during which he had not received any news from his government.

De Ruyter sailed past Iceland and then turned in a southeasterly direction. As he sailed just north of the Faeroe Islands he was met by a small Dutch vessel that immediately approached the admiral's ship. A messenger from the States General, De Ruyter realized. It had waited for the arrival of the fleet for just over fourteen days and De Ruyter knew from the serious expression on the captain's face that the news was far from exciting. War with England had broken out for a second time.

Van Wassenaar-Obdam's fleet had been defeated near Lowestoft losing seventeen ships. Even the admiral's vessel had exploded when a cannonball hit the supply of gunpowder and also De Ruyter's friend, the courageous Captain Kortenaer, had been killed.

"Gentlemen," De Ruyter began after he had called his captains together, "the news I must bring you will sadden you. War with England has broken out. Our fleet under the able leadership of Admiral Van Wassenaar-Obdam has been handed a serious defeat. The admiral is dead and so is my friend Kortenaer. Our fleet lost seventeen ships and has returned to our ports with serious damage. I need not tell you that we are not in a position to engage in battle although the navy of the enemy is looking for us. Therefore we must avoid being spotted and it is my prayer that we may reach our shores safely. I realize that it would be wise to seek shelter in one of the Norwegian fiords, but we are much needed by our fellow countrymen and therefore I have decided to sail for our own shores with the help of the Almighty. Be of good courage and place your trust in the hands of our God." Then he gave special instructions to each of the captains and ordered the small fleet to set sail again.

Staying close to the coast of southern Norway De Ruyter made ready to cross the Skagerrak for Denmark, but halfway between Norway and Denmark he met a merchantman whose captain warned him not to go along the Dutch coast since the English had posted a large fleet near the Dutch island of Texel knowing that De Ruyter would try to reach the Southern Sea, in order to reach Amsterdam.

"My lord Admiral," the captain of the merchantman said, "the English are sure that they can capture you because they know that you lack ammunition to defend yourself. May God bless you, Sir."

De Ruyter nodded. "Thank you, my friend. May the Lord be with us." He shook the man's hand and then returned to his cabin. His heart was ill at ease knowing that the English were swarming all over the North Sea hoping to take him by both surprise and force. In the quiet of his cabin he poured out his heart before Him Who is the Lord of lords and the King of kings, pleading with Him to guide him home safely so that he might be able to help his country in its hour of need.

At first it looked as if the Lord was not going to grant De Ruyter's wish. The summer of the year 1665 was almost over and it was early on a Sunday morning that the man in the crow's-nest shouted that the English fleet had come into sight. There was no longer a chance to escape. Soon the English would begin their attack and De Ruyter's fleet could not even defend itself.

The admiral stood on deck. Earlier he had given the command that each ship defend itself to the utmost but he realized that by so doing he would be responsible for the death of numerous fine men who were loyal to him. At the same time he abhorred the idea of surrender and would rather die at sea than be paraded in shame through the streets of London.

But just at the moment that the admiral concluded that everything was lost, the Lord graciously intervened. As if rolling in from nowhere came a sudden fog that separated the English from the Dutch. De Ruyter watched it with his mouth open in amazement. It seemed that the English fleet disappeared from the surface of the earth! Without firing a shot the two fleets passed each other, the one not knowing the whereabouts of the other.

What did the Lord have in mind with saving De Ruyter? The admiral didn't know precisely, but he thanked his Father for what He had done for his men and for him.

Three days later the fleet reached the mouth of the Ems River in the northern part of Holland. Staying out in the open waters would be dangerous for the English could easily attack, yet entering the river was dangerous since there were no pilots to guide the ships around the shallows. But De Ruyter had no choice. The Lord had guided him thus far, He would also protect him further. Ahead of his ships De Ruyter sailed up the river. His men were constantly measuring the depth of the water and the ships moved ever so slowly.

Without a mishap the fleet finally entered the harbour of Delfzijl. By God's grace, De Ruyter had brought his ships home.

The people of Delfzijl were overjoyed. When they had seen the fleet in the distance, they had been fearful, thinking that the English were about to attack the city. But now the word went around that it was De Ruyter himself who approached Delfzijl and by the thousands the people crowded around the harbour.

That evening the admiral allowed citizens to come aboard the ships. By the hundreds they came. Men as well as women were so excited that they embraced De Ruyter and kissed him. The admiral was overwhelmed by it all. The journey he had just completed had not been a successful one. That he had come home safely was because of the grace of God. What had he done to receive such a warm welcome?

The joy of the citizens was not because of feats accomplished. They didn't know what had happened around Africa and the New World. What made them happy was that De Ruyter had returned to fight the English, to drive them away from the entrances to the Dutch harbours and to punish them for capturing merchant vessels and for killing their crews.

"De Ruyter is home again! De Ruyter is home again! Not everything is lost! There is still hope, for De Ruyter is home!"

The news of the admiral's return also reached England. The secretary of Maritime Affairs, Pepys, wrote in his diary about his concerns now that the English navy had let De

Ruyter slip out of its hands. He foresaw that the Dutch admiral would cause the English a great deal of fear and worry again.

*       *       *

The news of the admiral's return had also reached Amsterdam where his wife had worried and experienced sleepless nights. Now she could smile again. A special horse and buggy would take her to Delfzijl to be with her husband.

She knew that she could be with him for just a short while. Yet every minute of it would be precious. The Lord had been good to her . . .

# CHAPTER NINETEEN

## *THE CALM BEFORE THE STORM*

While De Ruyter sailed from Africa to the New World and from there back to Holland, the Dutch at home kept busy building a new fleet. On the shipyards new vessels were being constructed, different in design from those built thus far. The English had been the first ones to change the design of their warships. The new English fleet had ships that were not only narrower than the older ones but also somewhat lower. This gave the English the advantage of having ships that were fast and could be easily manoeuvred.

The Dutch designs were different. Because De Ruyter preferred ships that were stronger in construction (wider and heavier) the government had ordered ships to be built that would meet the desires of the admiral.

Some captains felt that the English ships were better. After all, they were swift and could move even if there was just a bit of wind. Yet most agreed with De Ruyter. The English vessels tended to lean over when there was some wind and this would make it difficult to use all the cannons on board. De Ruyter's ships could endure heavy pounding and make better use of their cannons.

But they weren't De Ruyter's ships yet. During the absence of the admiral the command of the new fleet had been given to Cornelis Tromp. The young Tromp was very popular with his men and together they worked very hard at getting the fleet ready. But as soon as De Ruyter returned, the command of the new fleet was handed over to him. This made Tromp so furious that he resigned his position and went home.

However, when the States of Holland threatened to treat Tromp as a deserter, Tromp agreed to go with the fleet. He was young and didn't have as much experience as De Ruyter did. But in order to fight the English one needed the help of every brave man, and Tromp was brave and a born leader.

By this time the new fleet was ready to sail. All over the country people were waiting anxiously for what De Ruyter would accomplish. Many were sure that now the English would be thoroughly defeated and blown from the surface of the seas. Others were not so sure for they knew about the determination of the English. Would the English tolerate a little country such as Holland to stand in their way of being masters of the sea?

* * *

On September 8, the fleet set sail. But its first mission became a bitter disappointment.

The plans had been daring enough. The fleet was strong and for the first time De Ruyter had men on board of each ship who were not only capable sailors but well-trained foot soldiers as well. De Ruyter had planned to use them in an attack against the English. He would boldly sail up the Thames River, land these soldiers and have them destroy as much of the London harbour as they could. That would teach the English a lesson!

But it wasn't to be. Halfway between the Dutch and the English coasts an unsuspected storm surprised the fleet. The wind was so hard and the waves were so wild that it became almost impossible to keep the ships under control. A few collided with each other. Some lost masts and riggings. Other vessels capsized and sank. Without having even seen the English, the crippled fleet limped back to port.

What De Ruyter and his crews didn't know was that in England, and especially in the London area, a pestilence had broken out. People died by the hundreds, and sailors taken prisoner were set free to roam the streets to die from hunger and disease. For fear of having the pestilence spread to the navy, the English admiralty had ordered their ships to stay away from port. As a result, the English admiral saw his supplies dwindle, and his desire to meet De Ruyter shrank considerably.

During this troubled time in England the Dutch began the work of making repairs to their battered ships. De Ruyter received a brand-new ship named *The Seven Provinces.* It was a beautiful and proud vessel that would serve the admiral well during the days of his greatest accomplishments.

Refitting the ships took longer than was expected, but De Ruyter was convinced that it was time well spent. After all, new warships just had to be near perfect; the crews had to know how to handle them under all circumstances, and each ship had to do exercises with other ones before it could be trusted to function well in battle situations.

In the meantime, the pestilence in England had run itself out. This was good news for the English, but the bad news was that little money could be made available for the navy. Since many men had not been paid for some time, rebellious sailors took to the streets looting and creating unrest. Only then did the government make money available, a lot of money even, and rich citizens made large donations. No wonder, the news of De Ruyter's rebuilding the fleet had reached the English Isles and the people didn't like what they heard. Neither were the English too happy when they learned that the King of France promised to help the Dutch in their war with England. The Dutch themselves were cautious. Could the French really be trusted? Maybe not, but the English could not afford to take chances and found it necessary to send part of their fleet to the French coast just to make sure that the French didn't leave port to join the Dutch.

Around this time two important visitors wanted to meet the Great Admiral. They were two French noblemen, the Prince of Monaco and Sir De Guiche. Of course, the French were supposed to be the allies of the Dutch against England, although their fleet had not made a single move to show that it really was on the side of the Dutch.

The two gentlemen sailed as guests on one of De Ruyter's ships and were so eager to meet the admiral face to face that they requested to be rowed to his ship. They were sure that the admiral would be resting in his cabin and that he would not mind an unexpected friendly visit.

After they had climbed the rope-ladder and stepped on deck, they were both surprised and a bit disappointed. There was not an officer in sight and the crew was so intensely busy making repairs and doing their chores that they ignored the honourable guests. After all, welcoming visitors was the business of the officers and at that very moment the officers were enjoying their lunches.

Finally one of the boatswains approached the two noblemen. "May I help you, gentlemen?" he asked.

"We came to see the admiral," was their reply. "There's not an officer in sight to help us and eh . . ."

"The gentlemen officers are at lunch and the admiral is in his cabin, Sirs. We're rather busy, but allow me to have one of the crew direct you to the admiral's cabin." Then he called a nearby sailor, gave him instructions, and went back to his work.

The two gentlemen followed the sailor through narrow and dark gangways, up some stairs and down some other ones until they stopped at De Ruyter's door.

"Here it is, gentlemen," the sailor muttered. Then he turned and left.

"Strange customs these Dutch have," complained the prince. "Not enough manners, either. Somebody should have introduced us to the admiral. What do you think we should do?"

Sir De Guiche shrugged his shoulders. "We have no choice but to knock at the door," he replied.

The prince nodded. Then he knocked almost shyly. There was no answer although some faint sounds could be heard coming from the cabin. Maybe the admiral was pacing up and down, deeply in thought.

Again the prince knocked, a bit louder this time.

"Come in," a strong voice called from within the cabin.

Sir De Guiche opened the door and the two visitors entered. Almost immediately they stopped in utter amazement. The man standing in the cabin was the admiral alright, but he looked different from when the two had seen him before from a distance. The admiral was wearing ordinary sailor's clothes and stood there smiling while he leaned on a broom.

The Great Admiral sweeping floors?

"Just a second, gentlemen. I'm almost finished. You see, like so many others, the lad who keeps my cabin tidied up was stricken by the fever. If I don't help my crew get the work done, our ship will be a mess in no time." Then he bent down and swept the little dust pile at his feet on a dustpan and emptied it in a wooden box.

"Ready," he announced, while offering his visitors a chair. From the shelf he produced both cake and wine. In the meantime the Prince of Monaco began to praise De Ruyter in a flood of words that had the admiral flabbergasted. So much praise just for him?

De Ruyter shook his head while he raised his hand. He didn't want to be praised. "It is the Lord, gentlemen, Who grants victory either by a large fleet or by a small one. Don't praise me, but praise Him. I'm merely an instrument in His hand. Without Him I can do absolutely nothing."

Both the admiral and the visitors enjoyed each other's company thoroughly. When the Frenchmen stood up to leave, De Ruyter guided them to the door, picked up a bag that he had put there earlier, and put it under his arm. The Prince of Monaco raised his eyebrows. What did the admiral need that bag for?

De Ruyter guessed the prince's thoughts. "It's feed for my chickens, Your Highness. I love a boiled egg with my breakfast. You see, we've been too busy lately to feed them properly. So I'll tend to them now and then it will be my turn to enjoy lunch."

When a few minutes later the Frenchmen were being rowed back to their ship, they said very little. In their minds they were trying to answer a question. Who was this admiral whom the English feared, the man humble enough to dress like a common sailor, sweep his own floor, dust his own furniture, feed his own chickens, and who didn't want to be told that he was a great admiral?

* * *

The following day, as De Ruyter sat in his cabin without having closed the door, one of his officers came to see him. As he approached he heard the admiral speaking. Yet there was nobody with De Ruyter in the cabin. Then the officer realized that the admiral was in prayer. The officer made sure to remember every word said. A while later the man returned to his own quarters and wrote the part of the prayer he had overheard.

"Lord, give me a humble spirit so that I will not become proud when people praise me. Give me the strength to fulfil the task my country has placed on my shoulders. Grant me the courage of a lion and in so doing do not let me get killed, but spare me for the sake and the good of my country."

It was the prayer of a great man, praised by friend and foe alike, a man whose desire it was to serve his country in humility.

The very next day De Ruyter welcomed a royal visitor. The Prince of Orange, who was just fifteen years old and was to be known as Prince (and King) Willem III, stepped on board. The crew welcomed him with shouts of joy and everyone was excited having the young Prince with them. De Ruyter appreciated his interest and showed him around the ship while answering numerous questions.

The Prince didn't stay long, but his presence had meant a great deal to the morale of everyone on board.

Just a few weeks later the month of June 1666 brought balmy weather.

The fleet was ready.

And so was the enemy.

# CHAPTER TWENTY

## *THE FOUR DAYS' BATTLE*

The fleet was ready, but there wasn't a sailor or a captain who looked forward to the inevitable. War always is a terrible encounter between countries that ought to live in peace with one another. De Ruyter was a peaceful man, yet he knew that it was in the sinful nature of man to pursue his own selfish ambitions, even at the cost of the good of his fellow man. Such ambitions often lead to theft, robbery, and murder. When these horrible ambitions are those of the governments of nations, they often lead to war.

De Ruyter was convinced that it was his duty to defend his country against the ambitions of the English whose country was large, powerful, and determined.

As the fleet left the shoreline behind, De Ruyter summoned the crew of *The Seven Provinces* on deck. The men gathered around Chaplain Flockenius who would again lead in prayer.

"Lord, we are but small and weak, but Thou art exalted and omnipotent. Grant us the strength we need to do battle. If it be Thy will, grant that all of us will survive the battle that is about to begin. Should Thy way with us be different, grant us the life that never ends, which the Lord Jesus has gained for us."

As the chaplain continued his prayer, the lookout in the top of the mast suddenly yelled, "Enemy straight ahead!"

"Amen!" the chaplain said and immediately the crew went about its business. *The Seven Provinces* and all the other vessels of the fleet were ready for the battle, of course. But during a battle, men do not get a chance to enjoy a meal.

Therefore it was a habit to have a quick breakfast or lunch and then man the battle stations.

The crew was anxious. A year earlier, while De Ruyter plied the waters south of the equator, the English had thoroughly defeated the Dutch fleet near Lowestoft. Now the men wanted to turn the tide. If the Dutch would lose this battle, the English would swarm over the oceans of the world and destroy all of the Dutch shipping. Thousands of lives would be lost and the country would be tossed into poverty.

As usual De Ruyter had divided his fleet into three parts.[11] Vice Admiral Cornelis Evertsen[12] led the first squadron, De Ruyter the middle, and Cornelis Tromp the rear squadron.

While most of the men were having a quick meal, others raised the anchors hastily. Through his spyglass De Ruyter saw that most of the other ships did the same. Some were so eager to get into action that they cut off their anchor cables.

But there was also something that made the admiral frown. He knew that the English had rebuilt their fleet and that their new ships were strong and slender. Yet he was not told that they were very swift. Having the wind in their sails they approached the Dutch fleet at an unbelievable speed.

In the meantime the boatswains urged their men on. Those who were still trying to enjoy their meal gobbled their soup-with-bacon as quickly as they could, but the stuff was so hot that they just left their pewter plates half full.

---

[11] During the 16th and 17th centuries it was custom for fleets to be divided into three squadrons. Two squadrons were under the command of a vice admiral while the admiral commanded the third. Each flagship carried a huge white, red, or blue flag. This was to let captains know where the commander of their squadron was and what flag signals he might raise. During the "Four Days Battle," De Ruyter, Tromp, and Evertsen were squadron leaders, while Ayscue and Prince Rupert led two of the English squadrons. Admiral Monk commanded his own.

[12] A brother of Johan Evertsen. After the battle of Lowestoft, Johan Evertsen had resigned from the fleet.

Through his spyglass the English admiral George Monk, the Duke of Albemarle, had noticed that the Dutch had not counted on the great speed of his ships and that some Dutch crews were still cutting their anchor cables. That made them sitting ducks, he knew. Quickly he ordered his burners[13] to attack.

*George Monk*
*the Duke of Albemarle*

Monk's plan, however, didn't work. Part of his fleet had not been able to keep up with the newer vessels and the ships bumped into each other, causing some chaos. But Monk was a good leader. By means of flag signals he managed to restore order and to line up his ships in the same formation as De Ruyter had done. The English had copied De Ruyter's strategies!

At top speed the English sailed through the Dutch fleet with their cannons firing. Then they split their formation. Two of their three squadrons began to attack Tromp's flotilla. Tromp was first of all a fierce fighter. Although outnumbered, he caused havoc among the English. The first ship to catch fire and sink was English. So was the second. Even Monk's ship lost its masts forcing the admiral to continue the battle from another ship. Then he brought his ships together and turned against the other two flotillas of the Dutch. De Ruyter loved it. Monk made a big mistake that would cost him dearly. By means of flag signals De Ruyter manoeuvred his flotillas in such a way that they drove the entire English fleet between them and Tromp. Now the enemy had to endure cannon fire

[13] Burners were small vessels loaded with gunpowder. They would sail straight for an enemy ship and just before the vessels would collide, the gunpowder would be lit and the few sailors on board a burner would jump overboard and swim for safety. The burner would burst into flames, explode, and take the enemy vessel with it to the bottom of the ocean.

from all sides. Soon the first English ship lowered its flag, indicating surrender. Moments later another one. A third one was taking water so badly that it threatened to capsize.

De Ruyter paced up and down the deck encouraging his men or shouting messages to the flagman in the mast. As the day wore on, he realized that the English losses were severe and that the discipline among their vessels faltered. When evening came, the ships of both fleets stopped firing. Darkness made it impossible to read the flag signals that the admirals used to direct the ships, and the long hours of the night were needed to make the necessary repairs, to look after the wounded, and to bury the dead in the sea.

Early the next morning De Ruyter called his captains together. Before the battle would resume, he wished to speak to them. In sober, yet stern, language he reminded them that they should not fall back into the mistake of leaving the formation to attack a ship on their own. That mistake had left Vice Admiral Evertsen's ship unprotected and that was why this brave man had not only lost his ship, but also his life.

"Strict discipline, gentlemen. Nothing else but strict discipline. We used to attack on our own. It does no longer work. We must work like a team. Disobedience of even one of you may cost us the victory. You are dismissed."

By about eight o'clock the English began their attack once more. Michael De Ruyter could not help but admire George Monk for the tight discipline among his ships. The English worked like a team. They also realized that strict discipline was an absolute must. Looking at his own fleet, De Ruyter noticed that again his ships were not sailing in a tight formation and that some were crowding the others. Why was it, he sighed, that his own people found it so impossible to follow orders, and why was it that so many of his captains wanted to shine all by themselves? Why was it that even Vice Admiral Tromp could not submit himself to the leadership of his own commander?

Just as Monk was about to cut through the Dutch fleet, De Ruyter noticed that Tromp had raised signal flags ordering the ships of his squadron to break away from the fleet. In anger De Ruyter stamped hard on the deck. "The scoundrel!" he shouted at the top of his lungs. "Does he want to see us destroyed?"

Then he realized that the shrewd Monk had waited for a chance to separate Tromp's flotilla from the rest of the fleet. Immediately Monk's fast ships made a circle around Tromp and began firing wildly at him. Now it was a battle between two English squadrons and Tromp's single one. It left De Ruyter's two squadrons against the weakest squadron of the English and De Ruyter could have destroyed it completely. But it was obvious that Tromp was in trouble. The admiral had on numerous occasions told his commanders that they should come to the aid of those who found themselves in a dangerous position. In spite of the fact that Tromp was the cause of his own misery, De Ruyter immediately signalled to his captains that they should follow him as he hurried to set his vice admiral free.

The battle to free Tromp was fierce and merciless. Again Monk lost some ships of his already reduced numbers. But also Tromp suffered when his second ship in two days lost its masts and began to take water. Once more he had to change vessels and it was with great difficulty that his men rowed him to the doubtful safety of another ship.

*Cornelis Tromp*

This time it was the English vice admiral Ayscue who renewed the attack. Having learned from De Ruyter during previous battle engagements how to manoeuvre squadrons, he lined up his ships and sailed right through the Dutch fleet, cutting off both Tromp's and De Ruyter's ships from the rest of the Dutch fleet. Now all of the English fleet pounced upon the two Dutch vessels with the intent to destroy them completely.

But De Ruyter didn't have in mind to let the English succeed. At full speed and with all cannons blaring he fought his way through the enemy's encirclement. While so doing *The Seven Provinces* was hit hard time and again. The timbers cracked, the sails ripped badly, and the crew had to fight numerous fires that had broken out. Still the English could not stop De Ruyter and neither did they get a chance to sink his flagship.

"Carry on, men," De Ruyter yelled. "A little more yet and we'll be out of immediate danger!"

Just when he neared his own fleet again, Tromp's ship emerged from the thick cloud of smoke that hung over the water.

Minutes later De Ruyter raised more signal flags.

Attack!

Once more the two fleets passed each other. The battle was not quite over yet.

By four o'clock in the afternoon the English sailed away as quickly as they could.

After two days of battle De Ruyter clearly was the victor.

* * *

It was the morning of the third day.

The day began with a disappointment. De Ruyter had hoped that as usual there would be enough wind, but the sails hung loose and this would prevent him from chasing the English before they could reach the safety of their ports. He knew that Monk had been soundly beaten the day before and hoped that he would have a chance to make the victory complete.

The admiral stood on deck watching the sky. Yes, shortly

after noon the weather changed somewhat. At first there was only a bit of wind, but soon it increased in strength.

"Full sail!" he ordered. Maybe he could not overtake the bulk of the enemy's fleet, but he might have a chance to capture or destroy the ones that had been damaged.

Suddenly the lookout in the crow's-nest yelled, "Ships on starboard!" Moments later he hollered once more. "Twenty large vessels on starboard!"

Through his spyglass De Ruyter scanned the horizon. There they were, twenty English warships.

"Prince Rupert," De Ruyter said, and one could hear the disappointment in his voice.

Prince Rupert commanded a strong squadron that had been ordered to watch the French to prevent the French fleet from coming to the aid of the Dutch. But the French had shown no intention of helping De Ruyter and now Prince Rupert decided to join Monk. His help might as yet change the tide for the English. Should twenty big ships with well-rested crews be added to Monk's fleet, De Ruyter might find himself in an unenviable position.

"Prepare for attack!" De Ruyter's voice sounded strong and full of determination. "We're going after Prince Rupert!" he added. Now the Dutch fleet changed course, turning away from the pursuit of Monk.

Looking through his spyglass De Ruyter noticed to his amazement that Monk also began to change course. The Englishman obviously intended to join up with Prince Rupert's squadron.

But this was a mistake, a serious mistake! The English were now headed straight for the Galloper sandbanks! Their smaller ships would not be in trouble, but the larger ones, including those of their own admirals, would.

De Ruyter could not believe his eyes. Would the English be so foolish as to risk their fleet at this time?

Yes! Already Monk's ship stopped suddenly, stuck on the sandbars. Moments later the second vessel, that of Vice Admiral Tyddiman, got into the same predicament. And the third, Vice Admiral Ayscue's huge vessel, got stuck as well. Now all three of the English admirals were separated from their fleet and helpless, unable to properly defend themselves.

Tromp's flotilla, sailing the closest to the English, headed straight for the stranded vessels. Tromp loved every bit of it! Just imagine, Tromp capturing not one but three English admirals!

But it was not to be. The English were excellent sailors and knew how to rock their ships free from strandings. First it was Monk's ship that got free, then it was Tyddiman's. But the largest of the three, the beautiful *Royal Prince* of Ayscue, had run too hard into the sandbar and could not be set free until high tide came.

It never happened. Tromp let his ship dance at full speed around the *Royal Prince* firing at will. First the masts came down and then fires broke out. Because it was stuck, the *Royal Prince* could not aim its cannons and since Tromp's ship was smaller and lower, the effect of whatever cannon fire the

*Royal Prince* could lay were minimal. Just as Tromp was about to give orders to make ready for boarding, the *Royal Prince* raised its white flag.

Surrender!

Now the crew of the proud vessel rowed their little boats to Tromp's squadron. Vice Admiral Ayscue didn't look too happy when he was welcomed by a beaming Tromp. For the proud Ayscue the war was over.

By this time the sun had set. It had not come to a final battle on the third day, but the fourth day would be decisive. De Ruyter called his officers together to discuss his battle plan. Again he urged his captains to stick to the plan, to exercise strict discipline, and to watch carefully the signal flags that he would raise.

Then he dismissed his captains and went to his cabin. He knew that Monk now commanded more ships than he did and that many of the enemy's vessels had not seen action yet.

Before allowing himself a few hours of sleep, he pleaded with his God and placed the fleet and the country into the hands of his heavenly Father.

Early the next morning the battle continued. Both fleets sailed into and through each other a number of times, firing wildly both from ports and starboards with varying results. A few times the English managed to pound the Dutch. At other occasions it was the other way around. Once both Monk and Prince Rupert saw their ships encircled by the Dutch and receive a severe beating. Both times they managed to escape.

Tromp let his flotilla take the greatest risks. Although successful, his ships were beaten so badly that by the afternoon he had to remove them from the field of battle. This left De Ruyter with only two thirds of his fleet and gave the English a strong advantage.

It was hard for Tromp to leave the scene of battle. Earlier he had become very angry with De Ruyter. Tromp's men had succeeded in freeing the *Royal Prince* from the sandbanks and Tromp had wanted to tow the ship in triumph to a Dutch port, but De Ruyter had not wanted to hear of it. Tromp simply could not be missed and therefore the admiral had ordered the *Royal Prince* to be destroyed.

Now De Ruyter had to resort to a trick. He pretended that he was going to remove his fleet from the battle, but in reality he planned to wage one more strong attack.

The English, mistaking the movement of the Dutch fleet for an acceptance of defeat, spread their vessels over a wide area and began making repairs.

Suddenly the Dutch fleet turned around. With a strong wind in their sails they jumped on clusters of English ships. The groups of enemy vessels were spread out over too great a distance to allow them to come to one another's aid. Because Dutch ships were everywhere, the English admiral could not properly communicate by means of flag signals.

In sudden panic the English fled.

"Take what you can and destroy what you can," De Ruyter signalled to his captains. Soon four large warships surrendered to the Dutch. Numerous other ones just stopped fighting and lay still in the water, waiting to be captured.

Sadly enough the wind that had helped the Dutch also brought a fog so dense that lookouts could no longer see the decks below them. Continuing the rout of the English now became impossible. When a few hours later the skies cleared once more, the English had disappeared.

That evening De Ruyter's fleet caught up with Tromp's squadron. Once more the captains came together on the deck of *The Seven Provinces.*

The English had been beaten. They had lost over five thousand men who were either killed or had drowned. Three thousand were taken captive, including Vice Admiral Ayscue. Eight large vessels were captured, twelve totally destroyed. Of the ships that had managed to escape, a number could not be repaired anymore.

"And you ordered my prize to be burned!" Tromp shouted angrily at De Ruyter.

"Indeed," De Ruyter replied in a quiet voice. "The situation didn't allow us to do otherwise. We could not have continued the battle should you have left with the prize."

Then he ignored Tromp's continued protests and began to count the losses of the Dutch fleet. Four ships were burned. Two thousand men were either killed or wounded. The vice admirals Evertsen and Van der Hulst were killed. So were some brave captains.

"The Lord didn't allow us to destroy the English although He allowed us a great victory. A war isn't over until the last battle has been won, gentlemen."

# CHAPTER TWENTY-ONE

## *THE TWO DAYS' BATTLE*

During the first week of August of the same year, 1666, the two fleets met again.

The English had done an almost unbelievable job of renewing their fleet. From the moment their defeated ships had returned to port, the rebuilding had begun. Now, only a few months later, an almost new fleet left port.

The Dutch had worked hard at rebuilding as well, but they had lacked sufficient lumber and had to be satisfied with just restoring their damaged vessels. This clearly put the English in a better position.

Again De Ruyter had divided his fleet into three squadrons. The first was under the command of Vice Admiral Johan Evertsen, who after the death of his brother had offered his service to the States Council of Zeeland again. De Ruyter commanded the middle one, and Cornelis Tromp the third squadron. During the briefing before departure De Ruyter had outlined the battle plan. Once more the admiral had stressed discipline and urged his commanders to come to one another's help should this be necessary.

From the moment the English fleet came into sight things went wrong. Evertsen's flotilla sailed too fast, whereas Tromp had not shown any desire to keep up with De Ruyter. Evertsen didn't see the signals De Ruyter had hoisted, while Tromp just ignored them. Just as Tromp decided to catch up, there came a great calm that prevented his ships from gaining the speed that was needed.

To De Ruyter's chagrin he found that his fleet had lost its togetherness. This time Monk made good use of the situation.

He sent his largest ships between the flotillas of Evertsen and De Ruyter, and suddenly it became clear to the latter that it was the enemy's plan to single out *The Seven Provinces* and to destroy or capture it in order to do away with the one admiral they feared most. While Evertsen engaged in battle, Tromp sailed past and began to attack the rear part of the English fleet. In the meantime, the focus of the English was on De Ruyter and soon they had him surrounded and began to pound his beautiful ship. It was impossible for the admiral to defend himself against so many and he hoisted signals to Tromp to come and help him.

Tromp should have done so. Had not De Ruyter done the same thing for him during the last battle? But Tromp ignored the admiral's signals and continued pounding the English with great success indeed.

Why did Tromp not come to De Ruyter's aid? Was it pride? Was it jealousy? Or was it because Tromp could not stand the admiral and therefore pretended that he didn't see the signal flags that ordered him to help?

We don't quite know. Maybe Tromp was selfish, interested only in his own fame and in his own career.

The situation became rather desperate. De Ruyter called one of his trusted officers, Van Nes, to his side and said, "What's happening to us? I wish I was dead."

"I wish the same," Van Nes answered, "but one does not die when he wants to." Then both left De Ruyter's cabin. About one minute later a cannon ball ripped through the cabin, destroying it completely. The admiral looked at his ravaged cabin in amazement. "One does not die when he wants to," Van Nes had said. De Ruyter knew it too well. One dies when it was the Lord's time and not a minute earlier.

Now De Ruyter regained his determination. He would defend himself to the very end. Never before had he lost a battle. He would not lose this one either, if it was the Lord's will.

Looking out on the sea past the English ships, he saw that Vice Admiral Evertsen's flotilla was withdrawing itself from the battle. He took his spyglass to take a better look. Evertsen's ships didn't appear too badly damaged and could have continued their struggle with the enemy. But the distance was too great to read the signal flags that Evertsen's ship had hoisted. De Ruyter found the situation confusing and a feeling of great anxiety took hold of him. Why would Evertsen also refuse to come to his aid? But De Ruyter didn't know that although Evertsen's ships could still fight, Johan Evertsen himself lost his leg, from which he died, and the other men in command, Van't Hoen and Koenders, were killed as well. The only commander left was Tjerk Hiddes and he lay seriously wounded in his cabin.

Still Tromp's squadron was nowhere in sight.

On starboard of *The Seven Provinces* sailed the huge *Royal Charles*, firing wildly at De Ruyter's flagship. On port side it was the *Royal James* that tried to sink it. Caught in the middle, *The Seven Provinces* received blow after blow. One by one the masts became damaged. Just below the waterline a cannonball blew a hole in the hull and so much water began to stream into the hold that the mighty ship began to list badly. Three times in a row fires broke out. Then De Ruyter noticed that the English had sent an unmanned burner straight at him. Should that boat so much as touch *The Seven Provinces*, it would mean a total disaster.

Now some twenty sailors quickly jumped into a boat and rowed feverishly to the approaching burner. In spite of the fact that the burner was already in flames, some managed to climb on board. Through smoke and flames they dashed for the rudder and tugged it with all their might. Coughing and choking they pushed and pushed. Finally the burner began to change course. When it passed *The Seven Provinces* without making contact, the sailors dived overboard and swam for safety.

By now the sad-looking remains of De Ruyter's squadron drifted closer to the safety of the harbour of Flushing. *The Seven Provinces* had lost its masts and what was left of the hull was a mess of broken timber. Would the ship sink before it could reach port?

The English kept on firing. Oh yes, their two mighty ships were damaged as well. The huge *Royal Charles* could barely sail anymore, yet it kept on firing without letting down.

De Ruyter felt depressed. Could something bad have happened to Tromp? And what had happened to Vice Admiral Evertsen? "Oh God," he sighed, "can there not be one bullet that takes me away?"

But there wasn't one. The task that the Lord had given De Ruyter had not been completed yet. Not yet.

Not too far from port other ships came into sight. Captain Banckert, one of the remaining officers of Evertsen's flotilla, had taken command and now began to attack the English. His courage gave De Ruyter the chance to bring his ships into port.

Still Tromp was nowhere in sight.

The next day hundreds of people crowded the harbour. They stood quietly near *The Seven Provinces*. Some wept, while others gnashed their teeth.

Near the entrance of the harbour another crowd had gathered. They watched how Tromp led his squadron triumphantly to its mooring places. Then Tromp had himself rowed to *The Seven Provinces*. With a big grin on his face he approached De Ruyter.

"I have thoroughly defeated the English squadron and have chased its leftovers right into their port and . . ."

"You deserted me," De Ruyter interrupted. But Tromp ignored him. "I did well, I think. The English ran to save their hides. If your squadrons had fought as well as mine . . ."

"What then?" De Ruyter's face turned ashen.

"Then we would have won the battle!" Tromp continued with a grin.

De Ruyter almost lost his voice. He was so upset that he could barely breathe. "Are you implying that I did not fight well?" he hissed.

Now Tromp's arrogance took the better of him. "Is my admiral jealous of my success?" he wanted to know.

In total frustration De Ruyter stamped hard on the deck. "You did not stick to the battle plan. You were out only to gain honour for yourself. You're not a team-worker. You're the reason why we lost this battle!"

"Was it my fault or was it your incompetence?" Tromp shot back.

That did it. "Shame! Shame!" De Ruyter yelled. "You are nothing but a selfish man, that's all. During this battle you became a deserter! You've put your own honour above the wellbeing of our country."

Tromp looked around and noticed how a large number of sailors watched the bitter argument in silence.

"You dare to call me a deserter in the presence of ordinary sailors?" Tromp screamed.

De Ruyter did not respond to this. Instead he ordered, "Scoundrel that you are, get off my ship and don't you ever try to talk to me again! Go!"

Tromp turned around without saying a word. Angrily he pushed some sailors aside. Then he left the ship.

That same evening De Ruyter wrote a long letter to the admiralty about the battle and about Tromp's behaviour.

Later, the admiralty launched an investigation and found Tromp guilty of insubordination. In a letter to Tromp they let him know that he was fired.

On the fleet there was no room for a selfish hothead.

# CHAPTER TWENTY-TWO

## *TO CHATHAM!*

It was close to the middle of June in the year of our Lord 1667 that De Ruyter left port with a refitted fleet. English spies had reported to their superiors in England that the Dutch were both furious and determined. Usually the people of Holland were friendly, a bit loud at times, and easy going. But once one got them furious and determined, one had to be careful.

The spies had also reported that the Dutch were building a new kind of fleet. Not only would there be the large and heavy ships, there would also be squadrons with smaller and faster vessels. The news that the Dutch had been practising with these light squadrons, coupled to the reports that Dutch soldiers were constantly practising landings, had the English worried.

However, the English had other things to worry about. A most terrible fire had broken out in London and a large part of the city had burned to the ground. Also another pestilence had killed hundreds of people. English citizens were tired of wars and longed for peace. The men didn't feel like fighting anymore and were more concerned about what happened in their own country than they were about what the Dutch might or might not do.

What did the English fleet do in the meantime?

While the Dutch had been rebuilding theirs, English ships had sailed up the Schelde River in the southern part of Holland and had burned numerous merchantmen. They had also landed on the island of Terschelling, burned down one of its villages, and departed with much loot. Because the English had become tired of warfare, they began to withdraw their mighty fleet to ports on their east coast.

In the city of Breda in the southern part of Holland an English delegation had presented a peace plan to the Dutch, but the men of the Dutch delegation had shaken their heads. The English proposals were insulting. The English should not think that they had won the war.

Now De Ruyter was heading toward the English coast. As soon as he had covered half the distance, he called his captains together in his cabin.

His opening statement shocked everybody. "Gentlemen, we're going to invade England. We will sail up the Thames River and land near Chatham!"

The captains looked at each other in astonishment. Up the Thames? That's suicide! "The English have fortified the banks of the river. Their cannons stand aimed at our ships. English soldiers are everywhere. Sir, the English have sunk hundreds of their older ships to stop us. Sir, we don't have navigation maps of the Thames. Our ships will run aground. Sir . . .!"

De Ruyter had expected this. He listened quietly to the outbursts of his captains. Then he said, "We have two English pilots on board and they have promised to help us. We're going in with our light squadrons. We'll sail at full speed, gentlemen. Admiral Van Ghent will lead the attacking squadron. You will recall that he was a colonel in the army. He's the one who trained the soldiers and you had better believe me when I tell you that these men are the best."

"I still think it's ludicrous," one of the captains continued. But the other ones didn't say anything anymore since they noticed that De Ruyter was fully determined to carry out his plan of attack.

"The main fleet will stay near the mouth of the river, just to make sure that the English do not attack us from the rear. Another flotilla of lighter ships will cruise along the English coast to watch the actions of the enemy fleet. Gentlemen, we will teach the English a lesson!"

*   *   *

The attack was about to begin.

Ahead of Van Ghent's flotilla sailed the frigate *Agatha*. Soon Southend could be seen from starboard and Sheerness from port.

Sheerness was strongly fortified. De Ruyter didn't want to have a powerful fortification threaten him in the rear should he pass it.

"Prepare to attack!"

But the attacking ships had to be careful. Everywhere were sunken ships. Many of them could not even be seen since they lay fully submerged. And there was more. There were numerous barrels in the water that used to show the captains of ships where it was safe to sail. Of course the English would have now put them in different spots so the Dutch ships would run aground.

However, the English pilots shook their heads. "No Sir, they're still where they're supposed to be. It's safe to follow them."

Van Ghent was surprised. The enemy had sunk hundreds of ships in an effort to stop them and yet had forgotten to remove the buoys? Unbelievable, but true!

Late in the afternoon the tide began to run out and the wind changed, making it impossible to execute a landing. Darkness would fall soon.

"We'll resume action early in the morning," Van Ghent said. "But we've got to be on guard. At night it would be easy for the enemy to send burners at us. With our ships at anchor, we would be sitting ducks." Thus he ordered a strong detachment of men to stay in their sloops ready to approach burners should they be sent out.

To the surprise of all, nothing happened. No burners. No activity whatsoever. It looked as if the English were at a loss of what to do.

The sun had barely gone up or the bombardment of Sheerness began. Then some eight hundred soldiers jumped into sloops and rowed quickly to shore. Finally they would see some action! But just as they were about to attack, the English raised a white flag indicating surrender. That was an encouraging surprise!

The soldiers entered the fort to secure it and to find a place where the captured garrison could be kept under guard. In the meantime Dutch sailors from Van Brakel's ship began to loot the village of Sheerness. They were men from Terschelling who wanted to take revenge. Hadn't the English plundered and burned their village on the island?

De Ruyter refused to allow such deeds to continue. War was a matter between armies. Citizens should be spared and protected. He had given strict orders that absolutely no looting take place. To make sure that everybody knew that he meant what he said, he forbade sailors to go to shore and had Captain Van Brakel locked up.

Since Sheerness was no longer a danger, De Ruyter led the larger ships up the Thames. In the meantime Van Ghent led his squadron further up the river and into the Medway since it had been reported that a large part of the English fleet rode at anchor near Chatham. There were reports that the English had sent part of their crews home and this meant that Van Ghent would not have to face superiority in numbers should he attack.

But the captains of Van Ghent's ships hesitated. What if the spies were wrong? Would the English be so foolish as to leave their majestic ships not fully manned while winter had not even started yet?

Van Ghent found it difficult to get his captains to agree with him. The representative of the Dutch government, who was on board Van Ghent's ship, hastily scribbled a note to De Ruyter and had a small sailing ship deliver it to the admiral. "Come immediately," the note read, "our captains refuse to follow your orders."

The captain of the little boat quickly sailed downstream with the wind in his sails. He delivered the note and De Ruyter responded in haste. Because of the wind he could not sail up the river, so he had some strong sailors row him. But the current was strong and the wind unfavourable. It took him hours to reach Van Ghent's ship.

By the time De Ruyter stepped on board, the captains realized that they had better cooperate with their admiral. They explained their concern to him. The Medway was treacherous and had many shallow places. It was said that Chatham was strongly defended, and that the English had strung a huge chain across the river. No ship could get by that place. To make matters worse, the chain was defended by one of England's finest ships, the *Unity*. Chatham could not be attacked. The English fleet was safe.

De Ruyter listened to the points the captains made and said, "But we must attack. We shall attack." Yet it was not quite clear to him how the attack could be successfully executed.

Then Captain Van Brakel stood up. De Ruyter had ordered Van Brakel to be set free to receive his punishment for looting after the battle. Van Brakel was really a good man and he was honestly sorry for having disobeyed the orders the admiral had given.

"My lord Admiral," said Van Brakel, "I propose that you let me sail at full speed toward the chain. With enough speed the chain will lift the bow partly out of the water, but my ship will be too heavy for it. The chain will snap, no doubt about it."

De Ruyter smiled. He loved courageous men and Van Brakel was one of them. "Count on it that there will be heavy fire from the *Unity*," he cautioned. "It will be dangerous."

Van Brakel nodded. "I know, Sir, but we must and will succeed."

An hour later Van Brakel sailed up the Medway. The English fired their mighty cannons at him and caused quite some damage, but Van Brakel didn't return the fire since it might reduce his sailing speed.

Yet instead of sailing straight for the chain, Van Brakel turned toward the *Unity*. Close to the mighty vessel he fired at it with all his cannons. Then he brought his ship alongside the enemy vessel and had his men board it.

But the sailors of the *Unity* were in no fighting mood anymore. Without shedding any blood, the *Unity* surrendered.

Now the Dutch were really all fired up! Immediately a number of burners were made ready. Their captains had orders not to put their ships ablaze until the chain across the Medway had been destroyed.

They didn't need to wait long. Captain Van Brakel had offered to ram the chain and to break it, but while he was still sorting things out on deck of the *Unity*, another captain by the name of Jan Van Rijn sailed straight for the obstacle. The impact his ship made on the chain was so great that his ship was partly lifted out of the water. Then with a loud bang the chain snapped! The crew hollered in excitement. "This is it, men," Van Rijn yelled, "this is it!" Looking around him he saw numerous burners sail straight for the English fleet. Van Rijn's ship put the *Matthew* on fire. Soon other ships went up in flames. Also the stately *Royal Charles* with Monk on board was attacked. Monk ordered his crew to defend the ship, but the men panicked and jumped overboard. With an ashen face Monk surrendered. Then he was confined to his quarters while Dutch sailors lowered the admiral's flag and raised the Dutch one. Then they began lifting the anchors and an hour later the *Royal Charles* joined the fleet as a prize. And what a prize it was!

Another large ship, *The Mammouth*, cut its anchor cables and fled. The *Mary* was not so fortunate and soon burst into flames.

Now the fighting spirit of the Dutch knew no limit. "Let's bomb London!" they yelled. "Let's loot the city!"

De Ruyter shook his head. He had seen many battles and during the last few years his hair had grayed. Never had he allowed any cruelty. Never had he turned his cannons on defenceless citizens.

"We've completed our task," he observed. "The enemy has received a serious setback. Now it's time to go home."

Soon the Dutch ships turned around. Jan Van Brakel received the honour of taking the *Royal Charles* in tow.[14]

Soon the English, hurt and tired of the war, sued for peace. A treaty was signed in Breda following the Dutch victory at Chatham.

[14] Even today a part of this proud ship can be seen in the *Rijksmuseum* in Amsterdam.

On October 15 of the year of our Lord 1667 Admiral De Ruyter stepped on land once more. The war was over. For good, he hoped.[15]

Yet the peace he had longed for lasted only a few years.

---

[15] What De Ruyter did not know was that notorious men after him never succeeded in doing what he had done. The French emperor Napoleon dreamed of invading England. The German tyrant Hitler had visions of walking victoriously into Buckingham Palace. But neither could bring his dream to reality. It was the humble and peace-loving De Ruyter who came so close to London that he could see its houses in the distance.

# CHAPTER TWENTY-THREE

## *AT SOLEBAY*

Secret information reached the States General in Holland with contents far from encouraging. King Charles II of England had made a deal with the French to unite in an effort to subdue the Dutch once and for all. Neither England nor France could endure the fact that the Dutch continued to prosper and that their ships were seen across the oceans. Dutch traders still sent large numbers of ships all over the world to purchase goods that would make large profits in the seaports of Europe.

The information the Dutch spies obtained also mentioned that the English and the French had united their fleets and that they had left their ports. They would meet somewhere in the English Channel and sail for the Dutch coast. With Prince James, the Duke of York,[16] as their commander they would land a large force of soldiers and attack Dutch cities and towns. The English figured that the attack would be successful for, after all, the Dutch were powerful only on water since their army was small in number and poorly equipped. Besides, the French armies would, together with the armies of the German Republics of Cologne and Munster, invade the United Provinces from the east side.

* * *

---

[16] Prince James was a brother of King Charles II and later (from 1685-1688) King James II of England.

In the early spring of the year 1672 De Ruyter left port. He was no longer a young man. Like many other men of the sea he was plagued by arthritis.

He paced back and forth on the deck of *The Seven Provinces*. The combined English and French fleet was nowhere in sight and it looked as if the enemy was trying to avoid contact at all costs. It appeared to De Ruyter that the enemy tried to prevent a clash at sea and knew that a victory on land would be more likely.

One question plagued him. Where was the enemy's fleet?

After having searched the open waters, De Ruyter decided to take a look at the ports. Maybe the combined fleets were lying at anchor waiting for a favourable wind.

During the early morning of June 7 the admiral learned of the whereabouts of the enemy. With the wind blowing from the east, he now hoped to use the element of surprise.

* * *

The Duke of York and his French colleague Vice Admiral d'Estries were still soundly asleep when a French captain burst into their cabin.

"Wake up, Sirs," he shouted, "De Ruyter is coming!"

The rude wake-up call could not have come at a worse moment. Many of the sailors were on shore following some rather wild partying and had to be rounded up before they could be taken back to their ships, and this would take a few hours. Furthermore, their ships lay at anchor and raising the anchors and getting the ships battle-ready was also time consuming.

* * *

De Ruyter was ready. He had been studying the sky, realizing that the wind might die down. Maybe there was enough time left for an attack with burners. Then he gave his commands and his voice sounded determined and crisp, "Let the burners attack!"

Van Brakel, the courageous captain of the action on the Medway, led the attack with eighteen fast ships and eighteen burners. From his command station on *The Seven Provinces* De Ruyter followed the action. If the attack succeeded, the combined English and French fleet would soon be engulfed in flames!

But with the rising of the sun the wind suddenly died down. The light ships under the command of Van Brakel soon lay still in the water. They couldn't move. The attack had become a failure.

De Ruyter was disappointed but not without hope. Surely, the smaller vessels could not do much, but there was still enough wind to move the large warships.

"Attack! Raise the battle flag!" he shouted. His men followed the command without delay. Moments later the wind began to return. By eight o'clock the first cannons were fired.

The English and the French weren't ready yet. Through his spyglass De Ruyter observed the commotion on the ships of the combined fleet. But he also noticed that crews were being rowed back to their ships and this meant that the enemy would soon be battle ready.

"Zeger, that is our man!" De Ruyter called out nodding at the first officer. Then, with a big smile on his weathered face he pointed at *The Royal Prince,* the largest vessel of the English, the one that carried the flag of the Duke of York.

Although the admiral had not issued an order, Zeger understood. He just grinned and lifted his cap. "No problem, Sir. It shall be done." Then he took over the tiller from the second officer, let the ship make a sharp turn to port, and sent it straight toward the flagship of the Duke. As soon as the ship was within striking distance, De Ruyter commanded the attack to begin. With its cannons roaring and the soldiers throwing grenades from their positions on the deck and firing their muskets while lying on the yards high above the deck, *The Seven Provinces* made ready to bump *The Royal Prince.*

But suddenly *The Seven Provinces* changed course. "Zeger!" De Ruyter bellowed as he turned to his first officer. But Zeger was no longer at the tiller. De Ruyter saw that his trusted officer had been hit by a bullet and was lying on the deck writhing in pain. Immediately De Ruyter himself took hold of the tiller and corrected the ship's course. A few men quickly carried the stricken Zeger below deck where the ship's doctor would take care of him.

As soon as *The Seven Provinces* had passed *The Royal Prince,* De Ruyter pushed hard on the tiller, thereby turning the ship around. Now its port side would face the enemy and the men at starboard could reload their cannons. When this manoeuvre had been completed De Ruyter handed the tiller to the second officer and returned to his position in order to lead the attack. First he quickly checked on Cornelis De Witt, the head of the Dutch government. Although the poor man was suffering from arthritis so badly that he could not walk, he had gone with the fleet to witness the battle. Seated on a chair on the upper deck and propped up by pillows, De Witt followed every move of the ship with much interest. Six halberdiers stood nearby, ready to move him should it be too dangerous to keep his position.

*James II*
*the Duke of York*

In the meantime the Duke of York received some help. Two or three English ships tried to sail between *The Seven Provinces* and *The Royal Prince* to give it protection against the punishment that De Ruyter meted out, but although they succeeded in preventing the Dutch from boarding *The Royal Prince*, they could not outmanoeuvre De Ruyter who kept on pounding York's vessel.

At times the air was so thick with smoke that the men began to cough badly. They could no longer see parts of their own ships and didn't know exactly where the vessels of either friend or foe were positioned. And there was also the danger of colliding with the ships of their own fleet.

And De Ruyter? He was everywhere. He would throw a bucket of water on a burning grenade, shout orders to the captain of the soldiers, help load a cannon when one of the crew was hurt or killed, give instructions to the second officer and to the man in charge of the artillery. Then he would take his spyglass and check on the squadrons of the vice admirals Banckert and Van Ghent. He noticed that Banckert had drifted quite far to the south and that he was trying to do battle with the French fleet. But the French continued to avoid contact, afraid that Banckert would destroy them.

Then De Ruyter swung around to see how Van Ghent was doing. He noticed that far to the north Van Ghent was attacking the squadron under the command of Vice Admiral Sandwich. What in the world was Van Ghent doing now? With his small *Dolphin* he sailed straight for the enormous *Royal James* and yes, he rammed it! Undoubtedly he planned to board it! How could he ever hope of capturing the *Royal James* that had a crew of a thousand men? De Ruyter's amazement rose even further, for now Van Brakel sailed away from De Ruyter's squadron to give Van Ghent the help he so sorely needed! De Ruyter stamped hard on the deck, something he always did when he became excited. Look, Van Brakel rammed the *Royal James* as well. Its rigging got stuck in that of the *Royal James* and backing away became impossible.

De Ruyter was too far removed from that scene of battle to see what was going on, but he noticed that from Van

Ghent's ship a sloop was lowered and that it went at top speed toward *The Seven Provinces.*

A message, De Ruyter knew.

Soon the sloop came alongside. A young officer took the rope ladder and quickly came on board. With perspiration and blood on his face he met the admiral on the quarterdeck.

"Greetings from my captain, Sir, . . . our vice admiral . . . is dead," he stammered.

"Van Ghent . . . dead?" De Ruyter asked in shock.

The young officer just nodded.

Van Ghent, one of De Ruyter's most capable commanders. Dead.

"Tell your captain not to lower the vice admiral's flag," De Ruyter ordered. "I don't want the English to know." Then he ordered the young officer below deck for some food and medical attention. With long strides he returned to his post. Quickly he observed the situation of the battle. "Sharp to starboard!" he commanded. To his surprise he heard a familiar voice say, "Just watch it happen, Sir, just watch it happen."

De Ruyter turned around and smiled. Zeger had returned to duty, his head all bandaged up. With his able hands he pushed the tiller hard. *The Seven Provinces* made a sharp turn and once more sailed straight toward *The Royal Prince.* Once again *The Seven Provinces* rammed the port side of the duke's vessel. Anew the cannons blared and grenades burst into flames on the deck of *The Royal Prince.*

From starboard the English began to abandon ship. The flag of the Duke of York was lowered, but not as a sign of surrender. The *Royal James* had burst into flames and the Duke left to seek the safety of another vessel, the *Saint Michael.*

De Ruyter had Zeger turn *The Seven Provinces* away. Through his spyglass he noticed that Van Brakel had freed his ship from the *Royal James.* A short distance from the Englishman De Ruyter saw Van Rijn approach the *Royal*

*James* at full speed with a burner! In excitement De Ruyter stamped hard on the deck again. If Van Rijn succeeded . . .!

By this time the captain of the *Royal James* had recognized the danger his ship was in and he shouted desperate commands to bring it on a different course.

Too late! Van Rijn and his crew were already about to leave their burner. Quickly the fires were lit. Then the men went overboard. The burner hit the *Royal James* midships. Almost immediately fires broke out on the mighty vessel. The sails caught fire, the ship began to list. While its crew hastily left, the *Royal James* began to sink.[17]

Now De Ruyter ordered Zeger to change course. Some distance away a few of his ships were engaged in mortal combat with the English. They needed his help.

Just a few minutes later *The Seven Provinces* was back in the midst of the battle. Again the smoke was so thick that it became almost impossible to recognize friend from foe. Yet the ships kept on firing. De Ruyter ordered a sailor to raise a signal flag in the hope that his captains would see it. But the poor man who was to do it was felled by a bullet before he could put a knot in the rope. Immediately De Ruyter jumped forward and completed the chore. Then he reached hastily for a bucket of water when a burning piece of sailcloth fell near his feet. Yet at no time did he let even the smallest detail of the battle escape his attention. He knew that the English were beaten badly, although they were not totally destroyed.

When evening came, the English began to withdraw. "They need time to lick their wounds, Sir," Zeger observed. De Ruyter nodded. Certainly, the English were hurting, but also the Dutch had sustained much damage.

---

[17] The English vice admiral, the Lord of Sandwich, chose to remain on board and die in the flames. For a more detailed description of the battle at Solebay, see, Marjorie Bowen, *I Will Maintain* (William & Mary Trilogy, vol. 1) pp. 193-209.

The lieutenant of the *Royal James*, who had been saved by the *City of Groningen* and brought on board of *The Seven Provinces* was full of admiration for the Dutch commander. "Is that an admiral?" he asked. "He is an admiral, a captain, a mate, a sailor, a soldier, and a preacher. Yes, this man is a hero and all these things at the same time."

It was in these days, too, that Colbert said of De Ruyter that he was "the greatest captain who had ever been conceived."

After the English had departed and pursuit had become impossible because of the approaching darkness, De Ruyter summoned his commanders to *The Seven Provinces*. During the meeting he learned that the Dutch losses also had been numerous. His son Engel, captain of the *Deventer*, had been badly wounded in the chest. Van Ghent had been killed, and so had many others.

When the meeting was over and plans for the continuation of the battle for the next day had been discussed, De Ruyter stood up. His legs and hips were very painful.

As he slowly made his way to his cabin he realized how intensely tired he was. In his journal he noted that the battle at Solebay was sharper and of longer duration than any other battle at which he had been present.

Still, early the next morning he was on his post as usual. When the first morning light began to colour the sky, the admiral knew that the English had gone home, hurt too much by the battle of the previous day.

* * *

What about the French?

Already in the early afternoon of the previous day they had fled to their ports.

# CHAPTER TWENTY-FOUR

## *NEAR THE DUTCH COAST*

There were political developments in Holland that saddened De Ruyter very much. For many years the country had been a republic headed by John De Witt and his brother Cornelis. They had been fierce patriots and had done their best in the wars against England. But the brothers were unpopular with the common people who wanted the Prince of Orange to become Stadtholder, like his father had been.

As a commander of the Dutch navy De Ruyter didn't wish to take sides in the political conflict that ravaged his country. He respected the De Witts and yet he loved the Prince of Orange.

Cornelis Tromp had been different. This fierce fighter had never hid his loyalty to the House of Orange. From his masthead he never flew the Dutch red, white, and blue flag. His was orange, white, and blue. People had said that part of the reason why Tromp had been dismissed was because of his allegiance to the Prince. De Ruyter had not thought so for he, too, was a patriot who loved the Prince.

What saddened De Ruyter was that people had started to spread false rumours about the De Witts. It had been said that the brothers had betrayed their country. A huge crowd had gathered and tempers had flared so high that people broke into the jail where Cornelis was kept while John was visiting him, and murdered them. In the meantime, the twenty-one-year-old Prince was proclaimed Stadtholder and he wasted no time re-establishing law and order. But he also wanted to make sure that De Ruyter and Tromp became friends again.

The Prince needed both. De Ruyter was becoming old and would be retiring soon. Tromp was still young and the Prince felt that he was the logical successor to De Ruyter.

When the Prince tried to convince De Ruyter of the need of Tromp's return to the fleet, the old admiral showed his stubborn side.

"I have not been able to work with him, Your Highness. Tromp is very capable, but he cannot and will not subject himself to the commands of his admiral."

*William III of Orange (1650 -1702)*

But the Prince had proved to be very persuasive. "Cornelis Tromp is a good fighter, Sir."

"Too good a fighter, Your Highness, and for that reason he will not obey my commands."

"The situation of the country is too serious to leave a daring man, who can and will fight, at home."

"But, Your Highness, a good cooperation on the fleet is more important than shortsighted braveness."

"I agree, Sir. Good cooperation is necessary between you and me, but also between you and Tromp. The predicament of the country demands it. I want you to be reconciled with Tromp."

"I am always in favour of reconciliation, Your Highness," the old admiral responded, but he didn't sound very convinced.

William of Orange gave an order that Cornelis Tromp was to be brought in. In the presence of this great Prince — who, by the grace of God, had a year earlier, at great odds, saved the Dutch nation from utter destruction — Tromp promised to obey De Ruyter's commands and both admirals promised to help each other, to "put aside their former disagreements and from now on to live in a brotherly manner as faithful friends."

* * *

It was the year 1673, and once more England and France united in what they hoped to be the final effort to subdue the little country that had been a thorn in their flesh.

Since it was unwise to delay, the fleet set sail in May of that year although the Frisian squadron had not as yet joined. De Ruyter knew that the English and the French had combined their fleets and that they were heading toward the Dutch coast. Once more they would try to land and march their troops to the capital.

The English and the French had to be stopped.

Tromp had paid De Ruyter a little visit just before departure. "My lord Admiral," he had said, "It is reported that the French have most troops on board. Allow me to attack them. I know I can drive them right back to their ports."

De Ruyter had smiled. "You just do that, Tromp," he had answered. "You just do that."

And Tromp did it. Although the number of his ships was considerably smaller than that of the French, he went at them with the voracity of a mad dog. His initial contact had immediate results and the French began to withdraw. This not only separated the English from the French, it also separated Tromp from De Ruyter. Although Tromp hurt the French badly, because of their large numbers the French continued to send fresh ships into the foray. This made the situation for Tromp quite difficult and when at a given moment he saw his ship being attacked by some of the largest and most powerful vessels of the enemy's fleet, he shouted to his men, "Have no fear, De Ruyter will come!"

When he spoke these words he must have thought of the time that the roles were reversed. De Ruyter had found himself in a frightful position and Tromp had declined to help him. But he knew his admiral and he was sure that De Ruyter would come to set him free and to save his life and that of his crew.

In the meantime De Ruyter's ships were engaged in heavy combat with the English and although it was clear that the Dutch were the stronger, it took all of the admiral's skill and courage to keep the enemy at bay.

However, when De Ruyter received word that Tromp was in difficulty, he immediately ordered flag signals to be raised calling on the captains of his fleet to follow him. Without wasting time he went to the aid of the man he had despised at one time for not helping him when he was in trouble. "It's better to save your friends than to destroy the enemy," he said to Zeger.

Great was the joy on board Tromp's vessel. "Men, look!" Tromp shouted when he saw *The Seven Provinces* approach through the thick smoke. "*Bestevaer* is here!"

The battle against the French lasted into the evening. The Dutch lost only one ship whereas the French saw five of their best ships go up in flames. When darkness came, the French took to the shelter of their ports.

In the safety of his cabin the French admiral d'Estries wrote to King Louis XIV, "De Ruyter is a great master in the art of naval warfare. During battle he has taught me valuable lessons. I would gladly give my life if some of De Ruyter's fame could have been mine."

The battle was over, at least for the moment. De Ruyter's men worked all night making repairs to their ships and tending to the wounded. Just seven days later the combatants went at it again. This time the participants didn't strike at one another until mid afternoon and didn't stop until darkness had made it impossible to carry on. Again the English left the area to seek the safety of their own harbours. De Ruyter kept his fleet near the English coast to which the fighting fleets had drifted and spent time in his cabin to thank the Lord for having allowed him to again prevent the enemy from landing their troops on Dutch soil and for having granted him another victory over those who had sought his ruin.

In England the rumour went around that the Dutch had been squashed. The common people, tired of endless warfare, were eager to believe in their own victory. This mood of the country made it difficult to find men willing to join the navy. But this all changed drastically when, just three weeks later, De Ruyter's fleet once more sailed close to English shores. People began to wonder. How could the Dutch, who were supposed to have been defeated, manage to get another fleet together, and how was it that De Ruyter could sail by unmolested right in front of their own eyes?

The Prince of Orange and his government realized that the time and the opportunity to deal the enemy a complete and final blow now presented itself. On the wharves carpenters and shipbuilders worked feverishly at refitting the fleet. But, in June, when the fleet set sail, the admiralty knew that it was most certainly not as strong a fleet as was needed, even though this time also the Frisians had reported for duty. Yes, De Ruyter needed every ship available since it had been reported to him that a large fleet of richly-laden merchantmen was on its way to Dutch ports. Certainly both the English and the French coveted these prize ships. All they needed to do was put their navy between the Dutch merchantmen and the Dutch fleet. They hoped that by so doing they could dispatch part of their fleet to capture the returning merchantmen while the bulk of the fleet would keep the Dutch navy at bay.

To accomplish this, the combined French and English fleet tried to avoid contact with De Ruyter while the great admiral hoped for just the opposite, especially since he had been informed that also this time the English carried numerous soldiers with the obvious intention of finding a place along the Dutch coast where they could land.

The Dutch coast was not suitable for landings. The North Sea near the coast was shallow and the surf often treacherous. The most suitable place to land lay between the island of Texel and the estuary of the Maas River. Therefore De Ruyter kept on cruising up and down the coast in that area.

The Dutch admiralty realized that the returning merchant fleet could not break through enemy lines and that it was necessary that the enemy be chased away. Therefore the decision was made to instruct De Ruyter to attack. Prince William of Orange delivered the order to attack in person.

When an ordinary fishing boat took the Prince to the fleet, the crews of De Ruyter's ships had already decorated their vessels with flags and banners. When the fishing boat neared the fleet, the enthusiasm of the sailors knew no bounds. They began to shout and sing to show their allegiance. De Ruyter watched it with a twinkle in his eyes. His men were ready to do battle. They were eager to chase the enemy home once and for all.

After the Prince had climbed on board *The Seven Provinces* and had given the admiral the letter containing the instructions, De Ruyter gave a little speech to enthuse his men even more. While cannons barked their salutes, the Prince returned to the fishing boat. De Ruyter went to his cabin to familiarize himself with the instructions he had received.

The next day the fleet set sail to find the enemy. However, that same day storm clouds gathered. It began to rain and mighty winds made progress impossible. De Ruyter decided to wait out the storm and had his ships cast anchor. Three days later the skies began to clear and another three days later the enemy's fleet came into sight.

* * *

On the Dutch mainland near the coast church-bells began to toll, calling the faithful together for prayer. Everybody knew that the future of the country was at stake. Two mighty countries had banded together to destroy the freedom and the prosperity of a small country. The Dutch realized that without the Lord's help they could not successfully defend themselves.

* * *

At first the combined fleet tried to avoid battle, but on Monday, August 21, early in the morning, the battle began. Joost Banckert, the vice admiral of the first squadron immediately began to attack the French. De Ruyter, who commanded the second squadron, threw himself on the large English squadron under Prince Rupert while Cornelis Tromp raised the blood flag and went for the vessels of Vice Admiral Spragy.

The battle was fought so close to the Dutch coast that the thousands of citizens who had come together on the beach could watch the action. But around ten o'clock of that morning the Lord sent a heavy mist. Not only could the crowd on the beach no longer see the ships, the combatants also lost sight of each other. Only by clever manoeuvring did the Dutch succeed in staying on top of their enemies, causing especially the French to become quite confused. Just as the skies began to clear again, the French admitted being beaten by sailing as fast as possible away from the scene of battle. Banckert left a dozen ships behind to make sure that the French would not return, and with the bulk of his ships he turned around to help De Ruyter. Now Prince Rupert was caught between two ferocious attackers and suffered so much damage that he ordered his squadron to sail away to join Spragy's ships. These were engaged in mortal combat with the daring Tromp.

Tromp knew how to do battle and had the heart of a lion. With some of his ships he encircled Spragy's flagship and ordered its sails and timbers to be shot to smithereens. *The Royal Prince* sustained so much damage that it began to sink. Now Spragy was forced to abandon it and had himself rowed quickly to another vessel. One of his officers carried his banner and raised it on the new flagship. But again Tromp attacked and once more Spragy had to leave a sinking ship. The courageous man had barely stepped into a sloop to be rowed to his third flagship when a cannonball ripped the sloop apart. Vice Admiral Spragy fell into the water and drowned.

Nevertheless, the English were a determined people as Tromp found out. He too, had to leave his ship when it began to sink. Yet his flotilla had dealt the enemy a severe blow.

In the meantime Prince Rupert had great difficulty keeping his ships together. Time and again De Ruyter sailed his squadron right through the middle of the English fleet not only causing a great deal of confusion, but also inflicting great damage.

Some distance away and yet clearly in sight the French fleet had come to a halt. Frantically Prince Rupert sent signals ordering the French admiral d'Estries to come to his aid, but it was in vain. D'Estries stayed where he was and didn't move even after an English captain had personally delivered a note urging the Frenchman to join the battle. But d'Estries had seen enough. He declared the battle lost.

Now Prince Rupert realized that he had not been able to defeat De Ruyter. Disappointed and weary he sent coded signals to his captains. Within an hour the English fleet made half a turn and left the Dutch coast never to return again.

The English people, too, had had enough. In Westminster delegates from the Dutch Provinces and the English met to sign a peace accord. Also the German Republics of Cologne and Munster made peace with the Dutch.

On land, the fierce Prince of Orange recaptured the city of Naarden from the French and made a surprise attack on the German city of Bonn, forcing the French troops in Holland to leave Dutch soil. The regular day of prayer to be held on December 6, 1673, was changed into a day of thanksgiving through fasting and prayer.

The war, expected by King Louis and King Charles to be an easy victory, had turned into a humiliating experience for them, due, by God's grace, to the bravery of a young Dutch prince and an old Dutch admiral.

Back in his beloved country De Ruyter received nothing less than the greatest praise and honour.

"Too much honour," he mumbled during a festive ceremony, "too much honour. I was no more than an instrument in God's hand. All glory and honour belong to Him. The Lord accomplished this for us."

That evening he sat himself in his favourite chair near the window and smiled. Oh yes, his bones ached and he could barely walk. The arthritis and gout were so severe that he could barely raise his arms. But he was happy. Happy and very, very thankful.

# CHAPTER TWENTY-FIVE

## *THE HUNGARIAN PASTORS*

De Ruyter was happy to be home. Winter was approaching and it often sent stormy weather ahead of itself. The rain that seemed to have no end, and the boldness of the wind aggravated the problems the admiral had with arthritis. His legs hurt and at times also his arms and hands ached. He felt best when he stayed at home as much as possible and the warmth of the fireplace made him feel comfortable.

So it happened that most of 1674 he stayed in his home port. He would take short walks and enjoyed meeting friends again. He was an old man now and felt that his years of service had come to a close. It was good to be home, to be with his dear wife, to visit his children, and to be able to go to church every Sunday.

The following year started out in the same fashion, but then once more he received instructions to command a fleet.

The United Provinces enjoyed peace and was not hindered by either the English or the French. Its merchant ships sailed up and down the shipping lines undisturbed and once more prosperity returned to the Low Countries.

Just a few years earlier the States had made a trade agreement with Spain and this included mutual assistance in case of war. Now the Spaniards called on the Dutch to help them. King Louis XIV of France wanted to take the island of Sicily from Spain and a large fleet was required to protect the island. De Ruyter was summoned to take the fleet to the Mediterranean to help Spain. Also, should war break out in the Mediterranean, Dutch shipping would suffer. The Spanish

King, "considering Admiral De Ruyter the greatest sea-commander in the world" specifically requested that De Ruyter should come to his aid.

Of course, the admiral didn't just board his ship. He first went to the admiralty offices to check the papers of instruction. They informed him of the number of ships he would command, the names of the captains, and the supplies that he would carry. De Ruyter didn't like what he read. There wasn't enough of anything. He needed more ships, more men, and many more supplies. He also warned that the King of Spain could not be trusted and that the Spanish fleet was not worth much, while the French had a strong navy.

The gentlemen of the States General were not willing to listen. "I do not think, Sir, that in your old age you are beginning to be afraid and to lose courage?" one of them asked.

"No, I am not losing courage. I am prepared to sacrifice my life for the States, but I am surprised and grieved that the Gentlemen are prepared to risk and to sacrifice the flag of the States."

When pressed to go, notwithstanding his objections, De Ruyter finally declared, "The Gentlemen have not to beg of me. They must command me, and if I were ordered to go, flying the flag of the States on one single ship, I should put to sea with it. Where the Gentlemen of the States trust their flag, I will risk my life."

* * *

Michael De Ruyter was put in charge of an inferior fleet. As he was to step on board, he shook hands with a close friend. "My friend," he said, "I bid you farewell, not only farewell for now but farewell forever, for I do not expect to return home again. I will die on this journey. I feel it." Then he turned around and walked the gangplank.

It was on the first of January 1676 that the fleet reached Sicily and six days later the French fleet made its appearance. The Spaniards were nowhere to be seen.

De Ruyter had dealt with the French before. Their admiral, Abraham Duquesne, was a capable man and it was clear that he would try to drive the Dutch fleet out of the Mediterranean. He felt quite confident this time. His fleet was large and well equipped and he knew that the Dutch fleet was quite ill prepared.

*Abraham Duquesne*

Near the coast of the island the two combatants went at each other. Duquesne was a determined man, but he wasn't a strategist of De Ruyter's calibre. By clever manoeuvring De Ruyter managed to get the French fleet into an unfavourable position, and although the French fought with intense bravery, they were unable to overcome their opponents. Toward the evening Duquesne ordered his fleet to retreat.

By the time the Spaniards showed up the French were already on the run. The Spanish admiral who was appointed to the position of commander of the combined Spanish and Dutch fleet ordered De Ruyter to pursue the French.

"No," De Ruyter replied. "It is your turn. Your fleet is fresh and you should pursue the French. We need time to make repairs. As soon as we have restored our ships to be ready for battle again, we will meet you in the port of Naples."

The Spanish admiral nodded. He knew that it wasn't any use arguing with the fierce Dutchman and he'd rather stay on good terms with the Dutch admiral for he knew that he would need him in the battles to come.

So it happened that the Spaniards took it upon themselves to pursue the French, although De Ruyter knew that they wouldn't try very hard. When the Spanish king had asked the Dutch for their help, he had boasted about his enormous armada, the fleet of fleets as he had called it. Brand-new vessels of enormous size, he had claimed, equipped with the most modern guns and manned with experienced sailors. When De Ruyter was finally joined by the Spaniards, he was disappointed. The armada existed of a mere nine ships. "Bragging, that's all they do," he mumbled. "One cannot trust their words. It looks as if we are the ones who have to do the fighting for them."

He was correct. The Spaniards didn't display much of an effort to pursue the French and went straight to the port of Naples to wait for the arrival of De Ruyter's fleet of a scant eighteen ships.

When De Ruyter entered the port of Naples, he received a great welcome. Barely had he cast anchor when the Governor of Naples came to welcome him in person, followed by a large number of important people and many Spanish sailors carrying fruits and drinks for De Ruyter's men. The governor gave a long speech which most of De Ruyter's men didn't understand and presented the admiral with a gold chain, a portrait of the Spanish king in a frame of pure gold set with numerous diamonds, and a sword, the sheath of which was dotted with jewels. The festivities lasted into the late hours. When the Spanish guests left, De Ruyter returned to his cabin, where Chaplain Westhovius showed him two letters written on behalf of Hungarian pastors who were used as galley slaves by the Spaniards.

"The scoundrels!" the admiral blurted out. "How dare they treat me like a king while they keep my brothers in the filthy bellies of their ships!" Immediately he reached for pen and paper and wrote a letter to the governor who had just left his ship. "I demand that the Hungarian pastors be set free immediately," he wrote.

Two months later De Ruyter returned to Naples. He had received letters from the Governor that the Hungarian ministers would be set free. But upon further inquiries he discovered that they were still on the galleys. When the governor came to welcome De Ruyter, he was all smiles, but De Ruyter's face was far from friendly. He led the governor to the privacy of his cabin and closed the door. "Your Excellency honours me," he said, "by a welcome with many tokens of appreciation, for which I should be pleased. But Your Excellency should know that I cannot be pleased for all the honour given me, as long as my dear brothers, the preachers of God's Word, are sitting in bondage on the galleys and are being mistreated. If Your Excellency wants to do something for me and show me that he is favourably inclined to me, as he says, then let him free these miserable men from their bonds."

The governor swallowed hard. "It's not an easy matter, Sir," he began. "It's not easy. Only the King of Spain can give instructions to this effect. I don't have the authority to do this . . . so you really must ask him."

But when the Governor noticed the sadness of De Ruyter, he considered by himself, that His Majesty, the King of Spain would not like problems with this admiral. He then spoke, "Well, my lord, who would deny a request from such an Admiral, who is the defender and keeper of these countries. I will set them free! I believe that I am serving my king by granting you this favour, although it is without his orders. Their liberty is given you."

The Governor then ordered the Prince of Piombino, the general of the galleys, to set the pastors free.

Immediately the chaplains Westhovius and Viret went with three sloops to the galleys of the Prince of Piombino. The prince gave some quick orders and set the captured pastors free. There were twenty-three of them. They were brought to the ship of Vice Admiral De Haan. The next day Chaplain

Westhovius picked up one more pastor who laid, chained by a heavy chain, in a hospital for slaves. Finally he freed two more from a jail. After that, they were all brought to the ship of Admiral De Ruyter.

On the deck of his ship they were welcomed by the admiral himself. Once he saw the miserable condition the men were in, he didn't waste time by holding a long speech. He just said how happy he was for having been able to help them regain their freedom. "Most of you are of the Reformed faith while others are Lutheran. All of you are Hungarians. You wanted to know what you could do for me to show your gratitude," he continued. "Well then, when you come home, everyone in his own place, do your best to be one in faith and to become one even more. This would be the best gratitude you can give."

He turned around and quickly gave his orders. The men would be divided into groups of two and sent to the ships of the fleet for the best care available.

Then he went to his cabin to thank the Lord for what he had been allowed to do.

# CHAPTER TWENTY-SIX

## *THE LAST BATTLE*

De Ruyter sat on an easy chair on the upper deck. The gout and arthritis didn't allow him to stand for any length of time. The wind had died down almost completely and, although the French fleet could be seen, it would take hours before both the Dutch-Spanish and the French fleets would be within firing distance. The sails were hanging loose and the crews were just biding time. Of course, the fleet was ready for battle. The ships had been repaired, the cannons stood loaded, and the men had their weapons at hand.

De Ruyter looked around. His seventeen ships were ready but the Spanish were not. Yes, their ships were huge, but they had outlived their usefulness. The timbers were old, some masts were clearly rotting, and the sails had been patched up so often that it was easy to see that they might rip once a strong wind came.

The admiral took his spyglass and scanned the horizon. There they were, the French, twenty-nine ships strong. Another two hours yet, at least.

De Ruyter mused. During the last few days he had written some letters. The first ones were to his daughters. The youngest, Marguaritha, had married a young pastor. His son Engel was still single although he was now almost thirty years old. Like his father, Engel was a man of the sea. When he came back to port, he had no home of his own to return to and no wife to embrace.

The longest letter he had written to Anna, his wife. Should he come home after this journey, he would be seventy years old and that would be time to retire for sure.

"Enemy approaching, Sir," one of his officers interrupted the admiral's musings.

De Ruyter stood up with difficulty. His fleet was already in battle order.

"Zeger," he ordered, "go for the admiral's ship!"

"Yes, Sir!" Zeger responded. "Just watch it happen!"

Zeger was a man of his word. He let the ship come almost dangerously close to the Frenchman and then let it pass on starboard. Now the cannons boomed, soldiers threw their grenades, sailors fired their muskets. As soon as the ships had passed each other, Zeger turned the ship around and passed the Frenchman from port side. The cannons inflicted enormous damage to the enemy, but also De Ruyter's ship suffered. Fires broke out in different places, one of the masts snapped off and crashed on the deck not far from De Ruyter. Several sailors, who had been posted around the admiral, died in the battle. Although De Ruyter knew that a few bullets aimed at him had made little burn holes in his great coat, he remained at his station.

Then something terrible happened. A cannonball hit De Ruyter, ripping off his left foot and shattering his right leg just above the ankle. The impact was so great that the old admiral was thrown over the railing and crashed on the deck seven feet below. In consternation a few sailors rushed forward.

"Don't worry, dear children," De Ruyter said faintly. Then he lost consciousness for a few seconds. When he opened his eyes again, he calmly said, "The fall didn't hurt me. It's my legs. This old man shall never walk again, I'm afraid. Well, I couldn't walk that good anymore anyway. Take me to my cabin."

Strong and yet loving hands carefully lifted De Ruyter. Moments later he lay on his bed in his cabin. The doctor was there already and immediately began his work of bandaging the wounds. Since the battle was at its height, the chief surgeon, who was on another ship, could not be taken to De Ruyter until past midnight.

Although De Ruyter was in terrible pain, he ordered that the door of his cabin stay open to allow him to see what was going on. "Callenburgh!" he called, "take over. Attack, Callenburgh, and keep on attacking!"

Fighting pain and exhaustion De Ruyter prayed. "O God, help us. Graciously be with my officers and men. Grant them courage and allow them to overcome the enemy."

In the meantime, the battle raged on. Slowly the Dutch obtained the upper hand. By the time darkness had fallen, the French fleet fled, still pursued by the Dutch.

De Ruyter didn't sleep that night. The doctor had been unable to stop his bleeding and the admiral felt his strength diminishing. His mind was still clear and he called for his secretary. "I want you to write this letter," he said to the young man. His voice was still strong, but he stopped from time to time because of the flames of pain that shot through his body.

"It has pleased God Almighty to visit me with an injury sustained during battle . . . Thanks to God the condition of my wounds and fractures is quite good and I pray that the Lord will give His merciful blessing on my physician and grant me healing."

Just before the arrival of the new morning, De Ruyter began to develop a fever. Unknown to his doctor an infection of the wounds began to sap the admiral's strength.

When the first morning light of the day following the battle peeked over the horizon, Doctor Johan Mannard, the chief surgeon, came to see the admiral. With the help of two physicians he washed the wounds with brandy. Although the pain was incredible, De Ruyter didn't cry out. He bit his lower lip and let out the odd groan. He kept his eyes closed and his hands folded on his chest as if he were in prayer. Undoubtedly he was in prayer much of the time.

The next day the condition of the admiral seemed to improve. The fever was down somewhat and the pain controlled. When Chaplain Westhovius visited him and expressed his sympathy with the Admiral, De Ruyter responded, "This miserable body is not so important, as long as the soul is saved. My pain is nothing compared to the inexpressible pain and sorrow our innocent Saviour suffered in order to free us from eternal pain and misery." After this Chaplain Westhovius heard him pray, "Lord Jesus, Thou hast said that we have to keep our souls in patience. Grant me, Lord, whatever Thou commandest: grant me patience to the strengthening of my soul, that I may remain steadfast until the end. For patience is more victorious than strength."

While the sick admiral lay thus, he still remembered the wounded sailors and commanded that they should be helped as much as possible.

On the nightstand next to his bed lay his Bible, but he could not sit up to read it. Since he was a man who had always lived close to the Word of God, he had memorized large portions of the Scriptures. Lying on his back with his eyes closed, he now recited the passages he loved so much.

The fourth day became a sad one. The fever came back and the wounds showed clearly that the infection had returned. Doctor Mannard examined the admiral almost every hour. Then, late in the afternoon, he spoke to De Ruyter.

"My lord Admiral, can you hear me?"

De Ruyter opened his eyes. "Yes, I can," he said with some difficulty.

"I must bring you bad news, Sir. I know now that not the wounds but the fever will cause your death. You will not recuperate."

De Ruyter nodded, indicating that he had expected this prognosis. Then Doctor Mannard left the cabin.

The young officer who functioned as the admiral's secretary stood outside the cabin. He heard the admiral recite Psalm 63:

*O God, Thou art my God;*
*early will I seek Thee:*
*my soul thirsteth for Thee,*
*my flesh longeth for Thee*
*in a dry and thirsty land,*
*where no water is.*

Then the admiral motioned with his hand. The young officer understood what he requested. He left the cabin and called the crew. There they came, the captains, the officers, the soldiers, the sailors, and even the ordinary deck hands. They stood around the admiral's bed for a minute, then each one touched De Ruyter's hand as a fond farewell. Most cried uncontrollably once they had stepped out of the cabin.

Moments later the great admiral folded his hands on his chest. He now waited for his Lord to take him home. By His grace he had won his last battle.

"The last enemy to be destroyed is death," the apostle Paul wrote in 1 Corinthians 15:26.

Between nine and ten o'clock in the evening, his soul departed to be with Christ and await the day of resurrection.

# EPILOGUE

De Ruyter's officers decided that the admiral should not be buried at sea. They ordered the crew to melt thousands of lead bullets and cannonballs to make a coffin. The body of the admiral would be taken home. The physicians prepared the body the best they could and placed it gently in the lead coffin. The journey home could begin.

However, the French admiral De Quesne had other plans. He didn't know that De Ruyter had died but assumed that the Dutch fleet would merely sail home for repairs and fresh supplies. Some distance away from the scene of battle he lay in wait.

Callenburgh felt very uneasy. Since he could not outrun the enemy, he decided to fight his way through the French fleet and hopefully escape a disaster.

But it wasn't to be. The French attacked and now it became clear how much the Dutch had relied on De Ruyter. Three of the Dutch vessels and four of the Spanish fleet burst into flames and sank. Had the French not run out of ammunition, they might have destroyed the entire fleet.

What was left of De Ruyter's proud ships limped along. As they struggled toward the Strait of Gibraltar, a terrible disease broke out. Having been unable to take fresh food and water on board, the crews had been forced to drink stale water and eat food that had been spoiled. Hundreds of the sailors died within a span of just a few days. Also Doctor Mannard was struck down by the fever and a few days later also his body was buried at sea.

It was already late in the fall before the fleet passed Gibraltar. Spain needed to be rounded and then the dangerous journey past the French coast would begin. Would the French attack?

During a dull December day as the fleet passed Cape Quessant the Dutch were greeted by cannon fire. However, the French didn't inflict any damage and didn't send ships to attack. Also when Cape La Hoque was passed there was much cannon fire but again, there was no attack. When the same happened near the French port of Calais, the Dutch realized that the French had found out about the death of De Ruyter. Their cannon fire had been a salute to an old admiral they had learned to respect.

When finally on December 10 the Dutch coast came into sight Callenburgh learned that ice had blocked the entrances to all Dutch ports. He was forced to sail first to Wight and then to Portsmouth in England until a month later the final crossing of the return journey could be made. In the harbour of the town of Hellevoetssluis the coffin was loaded into a barge that would carry it over inland waters to Amsterdam.

But the rivers and canals of Holland were also covered with ice. The barge could not get any further than Rotterdam. Again the people had to wait for the ice to melt, but on February 12, 1677 the coffin was carried into the home De Ruyter had loved so much.

The admiral wasn't buried until almost a full year after his death.

On March 18, 1677 a large crowd followed the coffin to the New Church in Amsterdam. Sixteen captains walked behind the family, followed by four admirals. The ministers of the government and delegates from foreign countries, including England, came next. And then followed the crowd in untold numbers.

Thus ended the life and the journeys of a man who had served his country well, a man who had placed his life into the hands of his Heavenly Father.

Along the streets stood many of the simple folks and those who could not walk so well anymore. Some bit their lips while others cried openly.

"I am resolved to endure everything for my country as the Lord will see fit to bestow upon me," De Ruyter had once said.

His words had been fulfilled.

# *Letter of William Henry, Prince of Orange, to Mrs. De Ruyter.*

*With great sympathy, we were informed, from Your Nobleness' letter, as well as from other sources, about the death of the Lord Lieutenant-Admiral De Ruyter, and we regret the loss, as much as we estimate the merits of his person and his excellent qualities. Your Nobleness can be assured that whereas God Almighty has been pleased to take him from here by a glorious death, the State and we will always keep a very fresh remembrance of his long and notable service, and are prepared to show this at all occasions, for the good of Your Nobleness and his descendants. We remain,*

*Madam,*

*Your Nobleness' ready to serve friend,*
*G. H. Prince d'Orange.*

*From the army at Aalst*
*June 8, 1676.*

## *In the Ropery* [1]

*In the ropery he was found*
*Drove the wooden wheel around*
*Twelve hours of the day*
*But the heart of Michael Boy*
*Suffered grief, deprived of joy*
*Oh Nay, Oh nay, Oh nay, Oh nay!*

*As a deck-hand, quick and neat*
*Did he sail on Zeeland's fleet*
*That was the way to go*
*To East India and the West*
*Boy, that was the very best*
*Oh yo, Oh yo, Oh yo, Oh yo!*

*There rides Holland's Admiral*
*Many pirate's cause to fall*
*A man of fire and steel*
*It's De Ruyter on his horse*
*Victor of so many wars*
*At sea, at sea, at sea, at sea!*

Dutch text

## *Een Draaiersjongen*

by Anton L. De Rop

*In een blauw geruiten kiel*
*Draaide hij aan't grooten wiel*
*Den ganschen dag;*
*Maar Michieltjes jongenshart*
*Leed ondragelijke smart*
*A ach! a ach! a ach! a ach!*

*Als matroosje vlug en net*
*Heeft hij voet aan boord gezet,*
*Dat hoorde zoo.*
*Naar Oostinje, naar de West;*
*Jongens, dat gaat opperbest!*
*Ho jo, ho jo, ho jo, ho jo!*

*Daar staat Hollands Admiraal,*
*Nu een man van vuur en staal,*
*De schrik der zee.*
*'t Is een Ruiter naar den aard;*
*Glorierijk zit hij te paard!*
*Hoezee, hoezee, hoezee, hoezee!*

---

[1] *In een blauw geruite kiel* — translated by Roelof A. Janssen. Stanza 1 should be sung languidly, stanza 2 joyfully and quickly, and stanza 3 slowly and stately.

In The Ropery
Een Draaiersjongen
Tune: Michieltje
Music: A. L. De Rop *)
Dutch Text: Richard Hol
English Text: Roelof A. Janssen
1. In the rope - ry he was found; Drove the wood - en wheel a - round Twelve
2. As a deck - hand, quick and neat, Did he sail on Zee - land's fleet; That
3. There rides Hol - land's Ad - mi - ral; Ma - ny pi - rate's cause to fall. A
1. In een blauw ge - rui - te kiel Draai - de hij aan't groo - ten wiel Den
2. Als ma - troos - je vlug en net Heeft hij voet aan boord ge - zet, Dat
3. Daar staat Hol - lands Ad - mi - raal, Nu een man van vuur en staal, De
hours of the day. But the heart of Mi - chael Boy Suf - fered
was the way to go! To East In - dia and the West; Boy, that
man of fire and steel! It's De Ruy - ter on his horse; Vic - tor
gan - schen dag; Maar Mi - chiel - tjes jon - gens - hart Leed on-
hoor - de zoo. Naar Oost - in - je, naar de West, Jon - gens,
schrik der zee. 't Is een Rui - ter naar den aard; Glo - rie-
grief, de - prived of joy. Oh nay, Oh nay, Oh nay, Oh nay!
was the ve - ry best! Oh yo, Oh yo, Oh yo, Oh yo!
of so ma - ny wars At sea, at sea, at sea, at sea!
dra - ge - lij - ke smart, A ach! a ach! a ach! a ach!
dat gaat op - per - best! Ho jo, ho jo, ho jo, ho jo!
rijk zit hij te paard! Hoe - zee, hoe - zee, hoe - zee, hoe - zee!
*) The first stanza should be sung languidly;
the second joyfully and quickly;
the third slowly and stately.
Order Number: CMR Michieltje 01
Copyright 1996 by Church Music & Records
Box 154, Neerlandia AB T0G 1R0 Canada

***It Began With a Parachute* by William R. Rang**

Fay S. Lapka in *Christian Week*: [It] . . . is a well-told tale set in Holland near the end of the Second World War. . . The story, although chock-full of details about life in war-inflicted Holland, remains uncluttered, warm, and compelling.

**Time: 1940-1945** **Age: 9-99**
**ISBN 0-921100-38-8** **Can.$8.95 U.S.$7.90**

***No More Singing* by Norman Bomer**
***with colour illustrations by G. Carol Bomer***

No More Singing is a poignant allegory, beautifully told, that will move many children to an understanding that the aborting of our children is legal [according to the governing authorities]. As parents read this story to their children and explain the sad truth of abortion, conviction will grow in young hearts. As that conviction is strengthened and nurtured, it will draw us nearer to that day when protection is again restored to all children.

— Curtis J. Young

**Subject: Pro life** **Age: 10-99**
**ISBN 0-88815-566-2** **Can.$5.95 U.S.$4.90**

# Struggle for Freedom Series by Piet Prins

David Engelsma in the *Standard Bearer*: This is reading for Reformed children, young people, and (if I am any indication) their parents. It is the story of 12-year-old Martin Meulenberg and his family during the Roman Catholic persecution of the Reformed Christians in The Netherlands about the year 1600. A peddlar, secretly distributing Reformed books from village to village, drops a copy of Guido de Brès' *True Christian Confession* — a booklet forbidden by the Roman Catholic authorities. An evil neighbor sees the book and informs . . .

**Time: 1568-1572** **Age: 10-99**

**Vol. 1 - *When The Morning Came***
**ISBN 0-921100-12-4** **Can.$11.95 U.S.$9.90**
**Vol. 2 - *Dispelling the Tyranny***
**ISBN 0-921100-40-X** **Can.$11.95 U.S.$9.90**
**Vol. 3 - *The Beggars' Victory***
**ISBN 0-921100-53-1** **Can.$11.95 U.S.$9.90**